In The Chaotic Murmur

Of An Unclear Destiny

In The Chaotic Murmur

Of An Unclear Destiny

Željko Vujović

ARPress
ILLUMINATING IDEAS
EMPOWERING VOICES

ARPress
45 Dan Road Suite 5
Canton MA 02021
Hotline: 1(888) 821-0229
Fax: 1(508) 545-7580

Ordering Information:
Quantity sales. Special discounts are available on quantity purchases by corporations, associations, and others. For details, contact the publisher at the address above.

Printed in the United States of America.

ISBN-13:   Softcover   979-8-89356-186-9
                eBook   979-8-89356-185-2

Library of Congress Control Number: 2024904121

The title of the book was taken from the book of Fernando Pessoa "The Book of Disquiet", p. 257, Dereta, Belgrade, 2017.

TABLE OF CONTENTS

ABOUT THE CHAOTIC MURMUR OF THE UNCLEAR DESTINY OF ŽELJKO VUJOVIĆ

This hybrid manuscript contains many different genres, so it can repel the consumer (reader) and pull him in different directions. It also contains telegrams and scientific articles and reminiscences of the narrator as well as the writer, lyrics (folkloric and author's), verses... – from science to the expression of honest difficult personal experience, which is the subject of this book. It is not a classic novel, but rather a writing whose structure escapes any classification, therefore it could be published in fragments, and it does not have to be read linearly, but at will.

In order to make it easier to find your way around, the reader is already exposed to the register of personalities, as well as terms that are dealt with in this book, which can be of multiple use to him.

This book is of deep love, devotion, and respect for the author's late wife, and it can also be considered as a guide and practice on overcoming difficult situations in life. Investigating his own inner self, especially the unconscious part, the author clearly talks about emotional reactions in the modern, alienated world. Improvising his imagination, he talks about a microcosm, which can be anywhere, in which there along-standing injusticeso be dealt with. How?

Read it, and protect yourself with knowledge, it will certainly not lead you astray. And accept everything that life puts in front of you, be ready, and understand all sorrows, difficulties, and injustices as a game that you solve, so that you and others do not set boundaries for you.

Through these lines, in which immense sadness is expressed due to the loss of a beloved wife, the meaning can be better understood, because, as Željko Vujović emphasized:

Only the strength of your personality will lift you toward success and progress.

Therefore, let's strengthen ourselves by reading.

Marina Đenadić[1]

---

[1] Marina Đenadić works in the Belgrade City Library. She graduated from the Faculty of Philology.

REGISTER OF PERSONAL NAMES

DICTIONARY OF PHILOSOPHICAL TERMS

accidental - (lat. accidents = belonging) irrelevant secondary, what is irrelevant to a matter. The opposite term is essential, substantial, and essential.

accident - (lat. = belonging, which is added; Greek. συμ-βεβηκός). An accident (occasion, belonging) is such a being that presupposes another being that already has its basic being and for which it is further determination. Aristotle's first category of substances and accidents are correlative terms and cannot be understood without mutual relation. Although they are two different realities, the accident cannot even be understood without its natural ability to belong to substance. An accident is everything that accompanies a substance, determining it or indicating a change. According to Aristotle, material substances are determined by nine primary accidents: quality, quantity, action, relation-self, passion, place, time, situation, and habitus.

afficiate – (act on someone) excite, act, influence. In the theory of knowledge, especially with Kant, this term has acquired a certain meaning, according to which things affect (act) the receptive consciousness, which, being so excited, Characteristically experience these things.

apperception - means the process by which some already existing psychic structure or cognitive base adopts and becomes conscious ("assimilates") psychic, that is, conscious contents. The term changed its meaning in the history of philosophy. Kant distinguishes "empirical apperception", i.e. awareness of one's own "I" during internal perception, and "transcendental (pure) apperception", which consists in reducing conscious contents to "I" as a unity of a priori elements of the world ("transcendental consciousness")

a priori/a posteriori - Contrast first between propositions. A proposition is known a priori if it can be known without experiences about a specific course of events in the real world. However, it can be allowed that some experience is needed to acquire the concepts included in the priority proposition. Something is known only as a posteriori, and cannot be a priori. This difference provides one of the fundamental problematic areas of epistemology. The category of a priori propositions is highly controversial because it is not clear how pure thought, unaided by experience, can lead to any knowledge, and empiricism has always been concerned that this can be denied. The two big areas where this happens are logic and mathematics, so empiricists have usually tried to show that these are not areas of real, substantive knowledge that we have in these areas depends on experience. The first line attempts to show that all a priori propositions are in some sense trivial, analytic, or matters of notation or convention of language. The latter approach is particularly associated with Quine, who denies any meaningful division between propositions traditionally considered provisional and other deep-rooted beliefs that appear in our overall worldview. Another contested category is that of a priori concepts, which are assumed to be concepts that cannot be "derived" from experience, but which are assumed in any way of thinking about the world: time, substance, causality, number, and self are candidates. The need for such concepts, and the nature of the substantive a priori knowledge they give rise to, is a central concern of Kant's critique of pure reason.

apriorism - a set of labels of those philosophical teachings according to which some knowledge exists independently of any experience, and necessarily precedes it psychologically, logically, or transcendentally.

being - (*Gr.* τὸ ὄν; *Lat. ens*), that which is (id quod est): thing, object, reality, individual and concrete being that constitutes reality. The basic meaning of the term is "to be something", that is, a being is everything that can be attributed to being in any way, that which has being as a property. Being is the most universal concept and fundamental object of metaphysics, it cannot be defined by gender and specific differences. The concept of being as such (ens ut sic) is one and analogous, it expresses the ultimate abstraction and says only that something is, therefore it opposes nothing (zero), and includes real and mental beings (ens rationis). Real beings can be real and possible; real can be independent (substances) and non-independent (accidents); independent (substances) can be independent (God) and dependent (creatures). A thought being (ens rationis – an abstract logical entity that usually has no positive existence outside the mind) can be grounded in reality (eg space) or ungrounded in reality (eg nothingness). The absolute foundation of being is real, real, self-contained, and independent, and as such the original being, the foundation for all other types of being. Questions about being are studied by metaphysics (ontology).

being - (*lat. esse = to be*), the inner principle of being, that by which a being exists, gets existence, ontic (about what is) reason that a being is. Being constitutes the first and most intimate act (reality) of being, it internally gives the subject every perfection (excellence). Being itself (ipsum Esse) is that which is above all the most perfect: namely, it relates to everything as reality. Nothing, namely, has (its) seriousness except in so far as it is: therefore being itself is the seriousness of all realities, including the determinants themselves (ipsarumformarum)" (T. Akvinski, S. th. I, 4, 1 ad 3)

category – Kant interprets categories in such a way that he considers them to be forms of thought utilizing which we understand objects. They are pure concepts of reason. All categories are based on logical functions and judgments. Based on the thesis that categories correspond to types of logical judgment, Kant systematized categories as follows: 1) Quantity: unity, multitude, totality; 2) quality: reality, negation, limitation; 3) relation: inherence and substance, causality and dependence (cause and effect), community (reciprocity between what works and what suffers); 4) modality: possibility – impossibility, existence – nonexistence, necessity – coincidence. Kant's categories remain only in the subjectivity of thought.

the concept of transcendental categories - developed by Kant in his critique of pure reason. Kant argued that there are twelve transcendental categories, which a grouped into four main categories:

1. Quantity: unity, plurality and totality;

2. Quality: reality, negation, and limitations;

3. Realization: substance, causality, and reciprocity.

4. Model: possibility, existence, and necessity. According to Kant, these categories are necessary conditions for all human thought and experience and provide a framework for organizing sensory input into meaningful concepts and judgments. Transcendental categories enable us to understand the world and are based on prayer about it, but they are basic concepts that enable experience

causality - one of the central problem areas of metaphysics. Causation is a relationship between two events that holds when, given that one occurs, it produces, begets, determines, or requires the other; similarly, we say that once the first has happened, the second must also happen, or that the second follows from the first. However, it is not clear that only the events are causally related. Kant gives the example of a cannonball resting on a pillow, but which causes the pillow to be the shape it is, suggesting that states of affairs or objects or facts can also be causally related. In any case, the central problem is understanding the element of necessity or determining the future. Hume thought events were in themselves "loose and detached"; how then can we imagine the power one has to restrain others? It seems that the relationship is not perceptible, because all that perception gives us (Hume claimed) is knowledge about the patterns that events form, and familiarity with the connections that determine the patterns. It is clear that our conception of everyday objects is largely determined by their causal powers, and all our conception of everyday objects is largely determined by their causal powers, and all our actions are based on the belief that these causal powers are stable and reliable. But although scientific research can give us broader and deeper reliable patterns, it seems unable to bring us any closer to the "must" of causal necessity. Specific examples of causal conundrums, quite apart from the general problem of forming any conception of about what it is, include: how are we to understand the causal interaction between mind and body? How can the present, which exists, owe its existence to the past which no longer exists? How should we understand the stability of the causal order? Is reverse causality possible? Is causality a necessary concept in science, or is it necessary?

craving (desire) - (lat. cupiditas, desiderium), any emotional or mental tendency to possess something.

dialectical materialism - the dominant philosophical line of Marxism combines materialism as a comprehensive philosophy of nature and science, with the Hegelian concept of the dielectric as a historical force, leading events forward toward the progressive resolution of contradictions that characterize every historical epoch. The combination was perhaps first fully developed by Engels, in Anti-Diehring (1878). Human thought aims to reflect the uniform but contradictory character of external reality. Plekhanov and Lenin interpreted dialectical immaterialism as a hint that the nature of the world coincides with the ideals of the revolution and the intoxicating belief that history itself guarantees the victory of one's cause or the party proved to be one of the most attractive consolations of philosophy.

dualism is a philosophical belief that suggests that, in the world, there are two different substances, usually understood as mind and matter, or spirit and body. Dualism posits that mind and body are separate entities that interact with each other but are fundamentally different. In the context of the philosophy of mind, dualism is opposed to materialism or physicalism, which holds that only physical substances and processes exist and mental states and processes can be reduced to or explained by physical phenomena. Dualism has been the subject of debate throughout history and philosophy, with various proponents and critics offering different arguments and perspectives. One famous dualist was the French philosopher René Descartes, who famously argued that the mind and body are distinct entities and that the mind can exist independently of the body.

dissatisfaction - protest, indignation, remonstrance, disobedience, indignation, regret, confrontation, restlessness, resentment.

empiricism - a permanent philosophical line that tries to connect knowledge with experience. Experience is considered either as the sensory content of consciousness or as anything expressed in some particular class of statements that can be perceived to be true by the use of the senses. Empiricism denies that there is any knowledge beyond this class, or at least beyond what is provided by legitimate theorizing based on this class. It can take the form of denying that there is any a priori knowledge, knowledge of necessary truths, or any innate or intuitive knowledge or general principles that gain credibility simply through the use of reason, which is therefore fundamentally opposed to rationalism. An empiricist account of our concepts will consider that they depend on experience: "nihil in intellect nisi prius in sensu" (nothing in the intellect that was not previously in the senses). Some philosophers, such as Aquinas, held to this principle without denying that reason can grasp knowledge, provided it uses the materials provided by the senses. One of the main problems for empiricism is to accommodate how thought does not only arise from experience but provides us with categories with which thought does not only arises from experience but provides us with categories by which we can organize it. The necessity of such an addition (and its legitimacy) is the central theme of Kant's Critique of Pure Reason. Radical empiricism, as advocated by James, the standpoints that are implied in their organization are themselves the subject of consideration. Key problems for empiricism include avoiding the image that I know nothing but my experiences of the present moment (skepticism), delineating the legitimate basis of theory in observation, defending the view that observation is itself free of non-empirical elements, describing legitimate ways of using observation to construct a picture of the world, and explaining or explaining knowledge that appears to have no basis in experience, especially mathematical, logical, or other a priori knowledge.

epistemology - (Gr.episteme, knowledge) - Theory of knowledge. Its central questions include the origin of knowledge, the place of experience in the creation of knowledge and the place of reason in it; the relationship between knowledge and certainty, and between knowledge and the impossibility of error, the possibility of universal skepticism; and changing forms of knowledge that emerge from a new conceptualization of the world. All these questions are related to other central questions of philosophy, such as the nature of truth and the nature of experience and meaning. It is possible to see an epistemology dominated by two competing metaphors. One is a building or pyramid, built on foundations. In this conception, the job of the philosopher is to describe particularly safe ways of building, so that the resulting edifice can be shown to be sound. This metaphor favors some idea of a rationally defensible theory of construction (see also foundationalism, protocol statements). Another metaphor is that of a boat or hull, which has no foundations, but owes its strength to the stability provided by its interconnected parts. This rejects the idea of a basis in the 'given', the favored ideas of coherence and holism, but it is harder to dispel skepticism. The problem of defining knowledge in terms of true belief and fact began with Plato's view in the theater that knowledge is true belief plus logos. For difficulties see Gettier's examples. For further questions, see confirmation theory, empiricism, feminism, neutralized epistemology, protocol statements, rationalism, relativism, and reliability.

force – (Greek δύναμις), or power is the ability to act, everything that can act and produce an effect. Effective powers draw strength from the reality of substantial form.

form - the form, how various objects are directly affected by the sense organs. In the case of imaginary objects, the form represents the unity of signs created by the concept. In the case of objects directly affected by the sensory organs and in the case of conceptual objects, the form is always the working, unique principle that connects. It answers the "how" question as opposed to the "what" question. This is how we distinguish between the external form of an object and its internal form (structure). In contrast to amorphous (formless) material, we find shaped, formed objects in reality and thought. We are also talking about forms, forms of thinking, feeling, aesthetic, social, etc. forms. In antiquity, opposite to Plato, who understood ideas, as the essence of things, as "pure forms" that exist outside of changing reality, Aristotle transferred them to things themselves and they became principles, the essence of things. For Aristotle, form is the active principle, matter is the passive principle of things. Kant differentiates between the matter of knowledge and the forms (which are a priori) of sensitivity and reason that shape the matter of knowledge. Hegel did not divide matter and forms but understood them as a unity given in the self-development of the spirit. In opinion, we distinguish between content and forms of opinion (judgments, conclusions, etc.). The logic that limits itself to the examination of forms is formal. From a materialist point of view, form is indivisible from content, and vice versa. Also, the form is not in principle something essentially heterogeneous from the content itself. It is very wrong to reduce the form only to something external. Thus, the form of a work of art is one of the essential elements of a work of art, i.e. a kind of way of exposing one content, which makes that content special, and artistic.

formal principle – (lat. Principium; Greek ἀρχή = beginning, principle, origin, beginning), everything from which something emerges in any way. According to Aristotle, the principle is "the common feature of all principles, therefore, it is the source from which reality, or creation or knowledge originates" (Met., 1013 a). A principle expresses a beginning or an order without necessarily including the idea of a positive influence on the being of the derivative. In this sense, the point is considered the principle of the line, but not its cause. It can be said that every cause is a principle, but not every principle is a cause. The concept of principle is important and common in philosophy, which by its definition is concerned with the investigation of first principles, especially cognition and action; therefore, in tradition, the principles of battle and emergence (Principia essendi) and the principles of knowledge (Principia cognoscenti) are distinguished. Scientific principles or axioms are the highest principles of every science, which interpret their subject and their essential features, they are immediately evident and certain, and they serve for inference and proof, while they cannot be proven themselves, that is, their truth is known from their presentation of the theory. Characteristically, philosophers accuse each other of improper objectification of things, and in the history of philosophy, every kind of thing will at one point or another be considered the fictitious result of an ontological error.

knowing (cognition) - an internal act by which we present an object to ourselves, while the object is not an act but is presented by an act, which shows that knowing and knowing an object is not the same. The object of knowledge can be something purely possible (golden hill), something existing (family house), and even something unattainable (wooden iron). The object is not created by knowledge but precedes it. To know an object means to understand spiritually, it signifies the presence of reality in the consciousness of an intelligent subject. Cognition is an act or action that takes place in the mind, but the act itself and the object of cognition are distinct from the mind. If knowledge coincides with reality, then we are talking about the truth. There are two basic types of knowledge: intellectual and emotional; the mental depends on the emotional, and the emotional needs to be mentally integrated.

matter - the basic category of philosophy, especially materialism. Matter is that which exists in space and time and which can act on our senses by causing feelings, it is the general basis of the entire natural-historical existence and events. One of the basic questions of philosophy so far has been the question of the basis and essence of reality, and in the course of its development, it receives the most diverse solutions. Thales finds the material primordial basis and the primordial beginning in water, Heraclitus takes fire, Empedocles the four elements (fire, water, air, and earth) as the material basis of the world, and this view was maintained until the 18th century. Democritus understands matter as atoms that differ only in shape, size, and position. Aristotle sees matter as a passive principle of things, as opposed to form as an active principle. He generally accepted that point of view in scholasticism. With Renaissance philosophy, a new dialectical understanding of matter as an active principle penetrates. The great philosophers of the 17th century separated matter from motion. Materialists of the 18th century understood matter as self-sufficient, i.e. in unity with movement, which constitutes the essence of every conception of the first mover. In this sense, the concept of matter is also understood in dialectical materialism, with the difference that the last remnants of the mechanism have been overcome. Until then the appearance of Marx and Engels, the prevailing opinion was that there are the last immutable parts of matter. Dialectical materialism prevailed over those static concepts, leaving no possibility of absolute similarity to any material parts, which should also be understood dialectically, i.e. in eternal movement and change. Following all experience, both historical and scientific, dialectical materialism postulates the infinity of matter. Matter, therefore, cannot be identical to any of its concrete forms, because each of its forms of existence is only a transitory form, one phase of its realization. From the philosophical concept of matter, the natural science concept should be distinguished, which talks about what and how matter is composed, what its smallest parts are, etc., it talks about atoms, electrons, protons, etc., i.e. deals with qualitative and quantitative determinations of matter.

metaphysics - (from Greek με-τά and τὰ φισκεία = behind physics) Metaphysics, in the general sense, means the research of what is beyond experience. Metaphysics is the science of being insofar as it is a being, in so far as it participates in battle, i.e. it does not study being in its diversity and manifold relations, but rather studies being as being, that by which it is being. It is the study of the last causes, the first and most universal principles of reality. Therefore, metaphysics is the science of the foundations of being and its totality, which it studies starting from battle, looking for the first and most universal principles, which most radically constitute all things. Modern philosophers, starting with R. Descartes, Kant, and many others, did not make a significant contribution to metaphysics, but they often questioned its justification and the validity of its conclusions, as well as the very possibility of any metaphysics. Modern criticism of metaphysics starting with Kant, G.W.F. Hegel to M. Heidegger, often tried to give new solutions, but they were mostly epistemological and less ontological.

monism - a philosophical view that holds that there is only one fundamental substance or principle in the universe. According to monism, all things and phenomena can be reduced or explained by this one substance or principle. There are several different forms of monism. For example:

1. Materialistic monism: This type of monism believes that matter is the only substance in the universe and is everything can be explained in terms of matter and physical laws. According to materialistic monism, consciousness, thoughts, and emotions are nothing more than physical processes in the brain.

2. Idealistic monism: This type of monism holds that mind or consciousness is the only substance in the universe and is everything can be explained in terms of mental states and experiences. According to idealistic monism, the physical world is a manifestation or projection of the mind.

3. Neutral monism: This monism believes that everything in the universe is ultimately made neither of matter nor mental phenomena, but of some third substance that is neither purely mental nor purely physical.

ontology - comes from the Greek word for being, but is a 17th-century coinage for the branch of metaphysics that deals with what exists. Except for his ontological argument, there have been many priory arguments that the world must contain things of one kind or another; simple things, unexpected things, and so on. Such arguments often depend on some version of the principle of sufficient reasons. Kant is the biggest opponent of the view that unaided reason can tell us in detail what kinds of things must exist, and therefore they do exist. In the 20th century, Heidegger was often considered primarily an ontologist. Quine's principle of ontological commitment is to be the value of a bound variable, a principle that does not tell us what things the theory claims exist. These are the things around which the variables move in a properly arranged.

phenomenological property – manifests itself as what it is, a property of experience, regardless of whether or not it can be said to manifest itself.

pleasure - a pleasant feeling that varies from a feeling of mild comfort, through enjoyment to ecstasy. In psychoanalysis, it is a subjectively strong and shortlived aspect of enjoyment, accompanied by the relief of the tension of drive and the achievement of satisfaction. The entire psychic activity is determined by the pleasure principle. During life, from the earliest period, the objects of pleasure change.

perception - a word that has a double meaning: a) research method, b) sensory mental experience. As a research method, observation is careful and planned observation to learn about an event or an object. If something is an external object of perception, it is called external perception, and if it refers to mental experiences, it is called internal perception, self-perception, or introspection. As a mental experience, perception (or perception) is a unique set of sensory activities caused by an external object.

principle - (lat. principium; Greek ἀρχή = beginning, principle, origin, beginning), everything from which something emerges in any way. According to Aristotle, the principle is "the common feature of all principles, therefore, it is the source from which reality, or creation or knowledge, originates" (Met., 1013 a). A principle expresses a beginning or an order without necessarily including the idea of a positive influence on the being of the derivative. In this sense, the point is considered the principle of the line, but not its cause. It can be said that every cause is a principle, but not every principle is a cause. The concept of principle is important and common in philosophy, which by definition deals with the investigation of first principles, especially being, cognition, and action; therefore, in tradition, the principles of battle and emergence (Principia essendi) and the principles of knowledge (Principia cognoscendi) are distinguished. Scientific principles or axioms are the highest principles of every science, which interpret their subject and their essential features, they are immediately evident and certain, they serve for inference and proof, while they cannot be proven themselves, that is, their truth is known from themselves.

reason – (lat. ratio), what something is logically or ontically based on, which can clarify something. Everything that exists has a reason for its existence and therefore everything is either "a se = by itself" or "ab alio = from another". It is a primordial fact, it is known by dawn (as the beginning of a new possibility), not by definition, starting from something simpler or better known.

reasons/causes - When we act with a reason, is the reason the cause of our action? Is the explanation of an action by giving reasons for doing it, a kind of causal explanation? The position that it is not will state the existence of a logical relation between the action and its reason: it will say that the action is if it did not get its identity from its place in the intentional plane of the agent (that would just be behavior that cannot be explained by reasons at all). Reasons and actions are not "loose and separate" events between which causal relationships are maintained. The opposite view, put forward by Davidson in his influential work Actions, Reasons and Causes (1963), argues that the existence of a reason is a mental event, and unless this event is causally related to the act, we could not say that it is the reason for the action; actions can be performed for one reason and not for another, and the reason that explains them is the one that was causally effective in inducing action.

soul – (Greek ψυχή, Latin anima), the etymological meaning is related to wind, life breath, breathing (Greek ἄνεμος = breath, wind; or ἄναιμος = bloodless, bloodless). Soul means that inner principle by whose power a being lives and acts, it is the principle of consciousness. The human soul is man's substantial life principle. Christian philosophical religious thought emphasizes the difference between soul and body, understanding man as a combination of two principles, material (body) and spiritual (soul).

substance - (lat. substantial from substance = what stands below), denotes the constant and permanent content of each being, what constitutes its identity in time, despite the changes related to accidents. In metaphysics, a substance is a being that does not presuppose another being that would already have its basic being to be its further determination. A being that is. A substance of an intellectual nature is called a persona. The idea of substance is the fruit of inference, not of perception. The idea of substance does not originate from the impressions of sensation or the impressions of reflection. The word substance is just "a set of ideas united by the imagination, which we call a special name based on which we are able to remind ourselves or someone else of that set" consciousness – 1) a special experiential, happiness towards the flow of one's own experience, which follows that flow as knowledge about it, as its registration, attention, and supervision over it. Consciousness in this sense, as a superimposed experience ("act over act"), is not always equally present in our psychic life; many experiences take place on a single level, and some are only subsequently, retrospectively, learned in "memory" that consciousness had registered them. Th is is why we talk about more or less conscious, subconscious, and even unconscious experiences; 2) the same as experience in general, the totality of psychic processes, subjective life known only to an individual through self-observation introspection); 3) fundamental ontological category: subjective being, subjective form (way) of existence, which in different philosophical systems is given a different ontological meaning so that consciousness is determined: a) as the only, exclusive, universal form of being (subjectivism, idealism), b) as equal, comparative correlate to material (objective) battle (dualism); c) as one of the basic phenomenal modalities of a unique, self-indistinguishable (really „indifferent") battle (absolute, indifference, emergence monism); d) as a secondary, nonindependent dependent), evolutionarily conditioned manifestation of the primary objective (material) battle, "subjective reflection of objective reality" (materialism); 4) permanent spiritual presence of some normative motives, social, political, aesthetic, etc. principles, and aspirations ("popular consciousness", "party consciousness", "artistic consciousness"). In this last meaning, consciousness is often attributed not only to the individual but also to collectives, historical epochs, cultures, etc.

transcendental - according to Kant (in contrast to the previous Scholastic philosophy, according to which this term is equated with the term transcendental is that which enables all cognition. In other words, this term does not determine the objects of cognition, but rather its a priori conditions and possibilities, forms, and ways of cognition of objects. Transcendental is that which does not arise from experience but is before experience and so conditions it, enabling all real cognition. These are a priori cognitive forms of our consciousness and therefore, they are primary, irreplaceable you are the conditions of every experience and rational thought; in short, of every object of experience and knowledge of every object, in contrast to the so-called the psychological real subject of an individual; therefore, that general the subject which, independent of all individual subjectivities, connects all subjects in their unique a priori lawfulness. In the end, the cognitive theoretical procedure that examines precisely those a priori conditions of knowledge and trying to reduce and expose them to their characteristic importance is called the transcendental method. In the broadest sense, today what is called transcendental is what is connected with the conditions for the possibility of experience, that is knowledge.

transcendental idealism - a term Kant used to characterize one element of his philosophy. Kant tries to combine empirical realism, preserving the ordinary independence and reality of the objects of the world, with transcendental idealism, which allows in a certain sense objects to have their ordinary properties (their causal powers, and their spatial and temporal position) only because our minds are so structured that these are the categories we impose on a multitude of experiences.

transcendental aesthetics – the science of all a priori principles of sensibility. „Everything that pleases itself is beautiful, without interest in real existence and possession of objects."

DICTIONARY OF PSYCHOLOGICAL TERMS

ability is the executive ability to directly perform physical and mental operations with a valid outcome. There is a difference between general ability, which includes a wide range of different types of operations, with a more or less uniform level of performance in each.

the affective sphere of personality is an emotional response. spirituality is a broad and complex concept, which can be understood in different ways depending on the context and individual beliefs. At its core, it contains the need for meaning and purpose in life, as well as a connection with something greater than oneself. The focus of spirituality is inner peace, self-awareness, and personal growth. Practices such as meditation or yoga can help individuals connect with their inner self, cultivate a sense of calm and develop greater attention, presence in the world, and find greater meaning in life. emotion (lat. movement, movement, with the transferred meaning that the person is affected by some movement). The meaning of emotion is difficult to define. It indicates states and processes of feeling. It requires a subsequent label of love or hate, fear or courage, etc. Emotions are monitored bodily changes, as well as changes in visible behavior, with a general orientation of internal or external dynamics towards something or from something that is the subject of emotions.

belief is the acceptance that something is true or real without empirical facts or evidence. It can be based on various factors such as personal experiences, cultural traditions, scientific evidence, and philosophical arguments. It can be conscious or subconscious and can influence thoughts, attitudes, behaviors, or decision-making. It can be deeply rooted, shaping one's identity, worldview, and sense

the conative sphere of personality is the will and motivational processes. It refers to the dynamic characteristics of the personality, which lead to activity.

cognition is the process by which the subject becomes aware of internal and external reality and acquires knowledge about it. It takes place through perceiving, learning, remembering, imagining, discovering, thinking, judging, using language, and any other psychological processes. It is directed toward discovering the truth and everything else of them, as well as special, specific (special) ability, which includes one (narrower or broader) type of operation.

consciousness is a state of being characterized by feeling, emotion, will, and thought.

identity is a person's sense of self, individuality, and recognizable characteristics. It includes both conscious and unconscious aspects of the self. It can evolve through different life stages and experiences.

intuition is an irrational psychophysical function that represents unconscious perception and a type of unconscious understanding of certain contents. (K.G. Jung). The general definition, given by psychology, says that intuition is a process that provides a person with the ability to have knowledge about him and to acquire that knowledge immediately, without analytical thinking, and it represents a link between the conscious and unconscious parts of the human mind, as well as between instinct and reason.

the mental content of a person are different thoughts, feelings, beliefs, attitudes, and memories, which make up the psychological experience of an individual and influence his behavior. They can be conscious or unconscious and shape the way people perceive and interact with the world around them.

a metaphorical representation is a way of describing something symbolically or representatively, rather than using literal language. It is characterized by the use of a word or phrase to represent something else with which it is not connected to help the listener or the reader understands the idea conveyed more creatively or vividly.

memory is the process of saving experiences and connecting them with the present. attention is the concentration of sensory and mental activity on some special physical or mental content. It can be intellectual or sensual, as well as willful and involuntary. Its role is in the selection of contents that are taken into account to with reality.

perception is a mental process caused by and based on sensory data. A cognitive psychological function that enables the organism to receive and process information and for sustainable contact with external and internal reality. It establishes a relationship between the subject and reality. It represents the interpretation of the object. For example, the perception of the illumination of an object depends not only on its actual illumination (objectively determined by measurement), but also on the context of perception, especially on the psychological state of the subject. The difference in the perception of the same object by two or more subjects arises from different referential systems in individuals. together with their unconscious psychic contents. These conditions are not definitive. They are subject to general and individual changes. Accumulated human experience is an integral part of an individual and affects his perception.

psychoanalysis is a system of psychological theory and therapy that aims to treat mental conditions by exploiting the interaction of conscious and unconscious elements in the mind and bringing repressed fears and conflicts to the conscious mind through techniques such as dream interpretation and free association.

reason is the ability of insightful (logical, critical, wise) thinking, understanding, and reasoning. It denotes the higher cognitive functions of the human mind. "Rational" experiences are opposed to "irrational" ones (drives, feelings, aspirations).

spirituality is a broad and complex concept, which can be understood in different ways depending on the context and individual beliefs. At its core, it contains the need for meaning and purpose in life, as well as a connection with something greater than oneself. The focus of spirituality is inner peace, self-awareness, and personal growth. Practices such as meditation or yoga can help individuals connect with their inner self, cultivate a sense of calm and develop greater attention, presence in the world, and find greater meaning in life. emotion (lat. movement, movement, with the transferred meaning that the person is affected by some movement). The meaning of emotion is difficult to define. It indicates states and processes of feeling. It requires a subsequent label of love or hate, fear or courage, etc. Emotions are monitored bodily changes, as well as changes in visible behavior, with a general orientation of internal or external dynamics towards something or from something that is the subject of existence.

thinking is a mental, predominantly symbolic process, which is used to understand and introduce some order into external and internal reality. The opinion is everything that belongs to abstraction, understanding, inference, judgment, imagining, and remembering. Perception and sensory feelings do not belong to thinking but complement it. Opinion is cognitive, but it is significant influenced by feelings and will. When the cognitive influence prevails, we speak of thinking as the fulfillment of desires, which has an apparent logical structure but is, in fact, guided by the desires of the subject. neuroscience is a multidisciplinary field that focuses on understanding the structure, function, development, and pathology of the nervous system. It includes various scientific disciplines such as biology, chemistry, psychology, physics, and mathematics, to investigate the brain and its relationship with behavior, cognition, and emotions. From several subfields of neuroscience, we distinguish cognitive neuroscience, which investigates neural mechanisms underlying mental processes such as attention, perception, memory, and language, and neurology, which deals with the study, diagnosis, treatment, and prevention of disorders of the nervous system, including the brain, spinal cord and nerves.

BIRDHOUSE

Already on the seventh day, it rained
as if with me the whole world
was forgotten
but you smiled
and the sky smiled
at the same moment
And you flipped through your life
and the stars sparkled into my life
and then you kissed me
like a bird knocking on
your window

**I am celebrating the day of your love tonight in the
birdhouse, in the house for two**

And while I'm telling you about us,
you look at me and smile
because you know it all
Even though the days pass,
the birds still come
to our window

**I am celebrating the day of your love tonight in the
birdhouse, in the house for two**

Gabi Novak sings

Authors: Drago Britvić and Arsen Dedić,
Source: https://www.youtube.com/watch?v=0I2ckIXc7Zs
Licenses: [Merlin] Croatia Records (on behalf of Croatia Records), and 2 Music Rights Societies, Podgorica,

I APPROACH THE WINDOW THROUGH THE CITY WALKING AUTUMN

Forty years have passed in this apartment on the sixth floor. It's autumn again. I moved, for the umpteenth time, the curtain at the right end of the window. Before long, below, the "Đina Vrbica" Kindergarten building. The yard is fenced. Grass park with furniture. Slide, sand pool, metal bed with bars for children. They grasp the bar with their fists, hang above the ground, and move, using the strength of their arm muscles, from one bar to another. My three children finished attending this kindergarten a long time ago. I'm looking at him. It's hard for me to turn back and look around the apartment. I see her! I am aware of every detail of the apartment even when I am not in it. Living room. In the middle is a small, square, glass table, covered in disorder with several books and a notebook in which I write various notes, bills for used electricity, water, garbage collection, and apartment tax. In the corner of the room, a TV that I stopped turning on. I am fed up with what I have seen all these years, during which he did not move from that place, from that angle. Two couches against two opposite walls, two armchairs in which you can gently rock when you sit in them. On the wall, opposite the window, a shelf with books and framed photos. Three document drawers, and four cabinets, two at the top, and two at the bottom. In the lockers are binders with some documents, diplomas, and various certificates. Most of the documents have expired. They exist without meaning. There are also albums with pictures of events from life, which have passed, mostly, in these last forty years, my life and the lives of those who lived in this apartment. To the left is the dining room with a large round table, which I haven't used for its basic purpose in a long time. On the right, by the wall, the piano, on which the daughter practiced playing when she was a high school student. To the left of the dining room, is a classic kitchen, separated from the dining room by a wall in the form of a bar. In the kitchen, there is an electric stove, a refrigerator, a kitchen cabinet with a worktop, and hanging shelves on the walls, in which there are many dishes. I don't know how I would use it. My wife bought it and used it sometimes when she prepared festive lunches for our grown children. The kitchen leads to a glazed balcony, which I also stopped going out to. Sometimes, very rarely, it happens to me that I take a step or two for a short time. In the second part of the apartment, there are two rooms, a small hallway, and a bathroom in the middle. The room, on the south side, towards Lake Skadar and the Adriatic Sea, has access to a small balcony on which there are lines for drying clothes. I sleep in another room, on the north side, towards the hill of Gorica. It now has only one bed, two chests of drawers, and two bookshelves on the opposite walls of the room. The three-door wardrobe is in the right corner when you enter the room, leaning against two walls. It has a lot more wardrobe than I use. I don't know what to do with so many wardrobes. My movement in the apartment is, for the most part, limited to lying on the couch in the living room, opening the refrigerator, eating at the bar, washing the dishes superficially, and going to bed for a night's sleep. It invigorates me when I happen to take an hour's nap, in the afternoon, in that bed. In the front part of the apartment, there is a small hallway with a shelf for shoes on one wall, and across the street is a pantry with shelves on the wall, filled with objects, that I don't think I ever use. The utility room is dominated by a washing machine. I remember that I bought it a long time ago and participated in its assembly, but I personally never used it. My wife used it. Now I will teach you to use it. So far, that storage room has been the most useful for me to store my backpack with hiking equipment, hiking boots, and hiking poles in it. I'm tired of thinking that I should arrange, and clean the whole apartment and all the rugs in it. (10/19/2022)

◊

When you see everything, analyze, understand, and decide, you return to your apartment, memories live in it and all emotions live in it. You have to live, look forward to each day that comes, and of course, remember the past. Man must not be alone but surrounded by people, children, grandchildren, and society, with the definition of life: "Everything that comes, I'm ready for it!"

We are the threads that connect the unborn with the dead.[1]

FROM AURELIANO BUENDIA TO ĐURO AND MILEVA (HUNDRED YEARS OF SOLITUDE)[2]

"Macondo". Đuričkovići – a hamlet in Katunska nahija. Njegule, locality in Đuričkovići. Đorđije - Đuka Pejov! It is said that he was a standard bearer in the Battle of Grahovac and that his medal is kept inthe Museum in Cetinje. It is known that he had a son Đoko. It is not known who his wife was and which one, nor whether he had more than one wife, that is, whether he married more than once. Djoko, Djuka's son, married three times. His first wife was from Stamatović. Her name was not remembered, and the fact that she was from Stamatović was remembered based on the fact that one of Đoko's two sons, whom she gave birth to, said that the Stamatovićs were his uncle. Đoko's older son was called Jovan-Musa, and the younger Boško. Besides these two sons, she also gave birth to a daughter, Milica. This woman died too soon, while her children were small. Because of this, Đoko married again, to a girl whose name was Višnja. It is not known who she was from, but it is known, according to the story, that she was a beautiful woman. She braided her long black hair and wrapped the braids around her head. Face white and ruddy. Đoko's sons, immature boys, could not take their eyes off their beautiful stepmother. For some unknown reason, probably due to an illness, she too died quickly, so Djoko remarried, for the third time, to Stana.

It is not even known about the Stana from which she was born. Stana gave birth to a son, Mijajlo, and a daughter, Gospava. Gospava is married in Pavićević, in Bandiće. Đoko ended his life by death, in his eighty-fourth year of life. He was planting hay in stacks and fell, from one stack, on top of his head. His daughter-in-law, Milosava, the wife of his son Musa, said that he would not have died, like other people who die, if he had not died like that.

Đoko's older son, Musa, and daughter, Milica, moved to Metohija, near Pec, in the 1930s. Both had their own families and descendants. It is known precisely about Musa that he had two sons, Zaria and Veljko, and a daughter, Darinka. There are descendants from Zaria, but there are no descendants from Veljko and Darinka. Đoko's second or middle, son, Boško, was born in 1891. He was a year older than Josip Broz Tito, who had an insatiable hunger for structure. The distance from

² Gabriel García Márquez, "One Hundred Years of Solitude", Joint Edition, Executive Publisher IRO "Education" OOUR "Publishing Activity", Belgrade 1985.

Kumrovac to Đuričkovići is about seven hundred and fifty kilometers. Via Karlovac, Zadar, Split, Makarska, Herzegovina, from Kumrovac to Đuričkovići, can be reached by car in approximately eight and a half hours. It is not known that Josip Broz Tito ever visited Đuričkovići, nor the Njegule. He did not even come close to them. He neither passed nor was near them, but he did travel to India, Burma, China, Africa, and so on... It is interesting and very significant that Albert Einstein was two years older than Boško, and three years older than Josip Broz Tito.

Boško had a wife Draga, a native of Grupković from Glavica near Danilovgrad. Draga gave birth to a son, Đuro, and a daughter, Jovanka. Jovanka was married to Otaševići. It is an interesting detail that Boško also had a daughter born to him by an Argentinian woman. That was before he married Draga. He belly for bread in Argentina, together with his father, Đoko, for thirteen years, from 1910 to 1923. It is not excluded, it is even very likely that they fled there from "these mountains" because "they did not want to be bound in chains". Based on that, it is completely clear that he did not participate in either the First or the Second Balkan War. So he was not liberating the country from the Turks. The earth was liberated without him. He did not participate in the First World War either. He was not present at the Battle of Mojkovac and did not help the Serbian army retreat, through Albania, to Corfu. He was not even on the Lovćen front, so it can be said with complete certainty that he did not contribute, in any way, to the fall of Montenegro and the occupation of Montenegro by Austria-Hungary. In no way did he influence King Nikola to escape from Montenegro. Refugees, in general, flee their place of residence by personal choice. So, King Nikola escaped, from the occupied country, by personal choice. What is the difference between the words "avoid" and "escape"? He was able to "arrive and escape", but not to "exist in a terrible place". In this case, that terrible place is Cetinje or my native Njeguši. "Fear of life tarnishes the face often. Heroes are known through suffering."

Boško, even later, did not participate either in the famous Podgorica Assembly or in the Christmas Uprising. They did it all and it was all done without him.

Boško's son Đuro was an only son. Only son! Such a son is guarded and careful like the eyes in his head. All hopes are placed in him that he will prolong the species, that the series will not stop so that life can continue. Boško educated him as much as he could at that time, believing that school was very important for life. He married, Mileva, a native of Đurović, from Begovine, Kosovi Lug, Bjelopavlići. Mileva Milovanova! Milovan Markov, Marko Radoičin, Radojica Piletin And Milovan went belly for bread in Argentina. When he returned from Argentina, he separated from his father Marko, in Begovine, and bought a property in Mamućevina. Đuro and Mileva got married immediately after the end of the Second World War. At that time, Đuro was 19, and Milava was 17.

That's how, from Aureliano Buendia and Macondo, we "arrived at Đuro and Mileva".

Đuro and Mileva lived in an indissoluble marriage for 53 years. They were separated by Đuro's death in 1998. The rest are their descendants. One branch of their descendants is shown in the following picture. The other two branches, from daughter Lidija, born in 1954, and son Dejan, born in 1958, can be traced to Lidija and Dejan.

DESCENDANTS OF ĐURO AND MILEVA –
ONE BRANCH OF THE FAMILY TREE

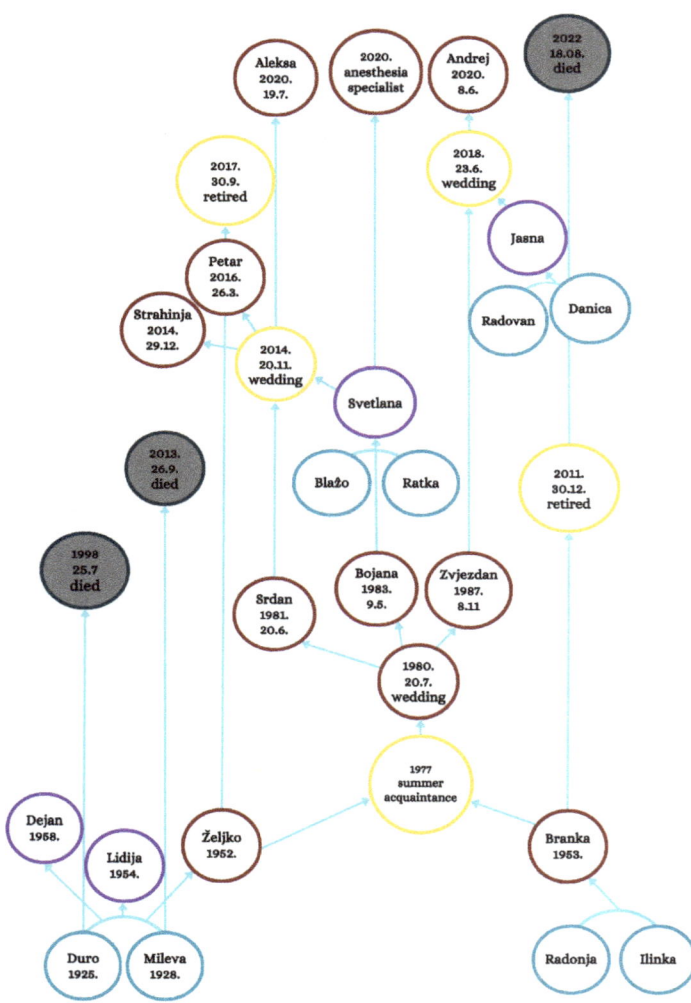

FOR MEMORY AND LONG REMEMBRANCE

Elijah of Thunder reads the biography of his father, in the "Memorial of the Historical Institute 1948 - 2018", page 371. He focused on the sentence: "From 1948 he lived in Titograd, where until December 1960 he worked as a journalist and editor of Radio Titograd, an employee of the People's Committee of Titograd, and an official in in the Republican Council of Trade Unions".

In the mentioned text, for an unknown reason, it was omitted that his father, from 07.01.1949. until 02.10.1949. "beating stone" on the Naked Island. Elijah found this information in the "Dossier: Naked Island", source: State Secretariat for Internal Affairs of the Republic of Croatia, State Security Administration - II Department, Zagreb, Assistant Head of II Administration, Jure Košutić. no. 1594, 4.IV1963. (surnames beginning with the letter N to the letter Ž): - LIST OF PRISONERS OF NAKED ISLAND, p. 113, 55th from top, 3rd from bottom, VUJOVIĆ BOŠKA ĐURO. "Authority is based on two things: containment and deception."[3]

What was the 23-year-old journalist of Radio Titograd, who graduated from teacher's school, hiding, and how did he threaten state security, to be arrested and imprisoned on Naked Island? Elijah, still a boy, asked him about it, and his father answered: "Nothing." The police searched the apartment of his cousin Drago Grupković, a native of Glavica on the outskirts of Danilovgrad, who could have been a student because he was twenty years old at the time, they found some list with Đuro's name, Elijah's father. That was the why and motive. Late in the evening on January 7, 1949, the police broke into the apartment where he lived with Elijah's mother, in one of the houses in the upper part of Njegoš's Street, towards Gorica, and took him away. He was arrested by Tripo Syndik, who lived in the building at the intersection of Marko Miljanov and Ivan Crnojević streets. Ivan Crnojević used to be called Moše Pijade's Street. Njegoš's Street and Marko Miljanov's Street are parallel to each other. Between them, in the middle, is Freedom Street. Elijah does not know what Tripo Syndik was by profession and what did he do? Elijah's mother and closest relatives (parents, father-in-law, and mother-in-law) did not know what happened to him, where he was taken, and where he was for a long time.

Later, it is not known how they found out that he was imprisoned in Bileća, and from there he was taken to Naked Island. The state of

---

3   Fernando Pessoa, "The book of restlessness", Derata, Belgrade, 2017, p. 485

workers and peasants found him the optimal place and conditions for work, personal spiritual development, and advancement" in the profession, especially and additionally "for the development of the family, the expansion of the family, so that the series does not stop, that life continues".

It is not recorded whether he performed the duties of chamberlain there, which is hard to believe because they were much older and more experienced than him, and therefore more deserving of that position.

So, in all likelihood, he was only forced to „beat the stone". The People's Republic of Montenegro was very nice to him in his life, education, and work in the institutions of the same country. It is stated in the literature that it achieved this through the technique of monitoring and eavesdropping, in an institution called UDBA.

UDBA was part of the Ministry of Internal Affairs (and that The ministry is part of the Government). The Prime Minister of the People's Republic of Montenegro, from April 17, 1945, to April 4, 1953, was Blažo Jovanović. So, on January 7, 1949, when Elijah's father was arrested, the prime minister was Blažo Jovanović, who was 42 years old at the time. The Minister of Internal Affairs, in that Government, was a thirty-year-old, normally operated on metaphysics, a Running Pissing Man, born in Gajeta. From the house of Elijah's father, that is, Elijah's grandfather, in Donji Zagarač to the house of Blažo Jovanović under Velje Brdo, there is a three to five-kilometer straight line.

Grandma of Elijah of Thunder used to go on foot from her estate in Donji Zagarač to Titograd, along the old Titograd - Danilovgrad road. She was leading a mare behind her, which she held by the bridle so that she wouldn't break away. There was a stall on the mare, and on both sides of the stall, there were baskets full of grapes and figs, harvested on the estate, intended for the son, daughter-in-law, and their children. She would arrange for Elijah to sit comfortably between the saddles, on top of the saddle, and ride like that. Whenever they passed under, Velje Brdo on that road, near Titograd, Grandma never missed an opportunity to point her head at Elijah and say: "This is Blažo Jovanović's house."

It is approximately fifteen kilometers from Blažo Jovanović's house under Velje Brdo to Glavica near Danilovgrad, by a direct route through the Bjelopavlić plain. It is approximately the same if you turn, near Stologlav, via Spuž and Martinići. It is not recorded that Blažo Jovanović never passed through Glavica, nor did he approach the Grupković family.

In the State Archives of Montenegro, Elijah sought information about „stone-pounding" Naked Island. Very interesting and more than significant, this information does not exist in the State Archives of Montenegro. This was confirmed by Lazar Kapisoda, head of the Central Depot of the State Archives. In other words, equal People's Republic of Montenegro and its „equal" government did not even know who and why they were arrested in Montenegro.

◊

Are such trademarks transmitted through generations? What will we do with those traces of inhumanity? How do we neutralize them? Although this is the only certainty, that hurts a lot, it does not mean that it should not be resisted - and finality and sadness! Has the time come that this former trademark is now considered an honor? Orwell's 1984, it seems, has not yet been published, and even if it had, would it have changed anything?

"The main order in a despotic society is you can't, in totalitarianism, you must, and the consumer order is what you need."

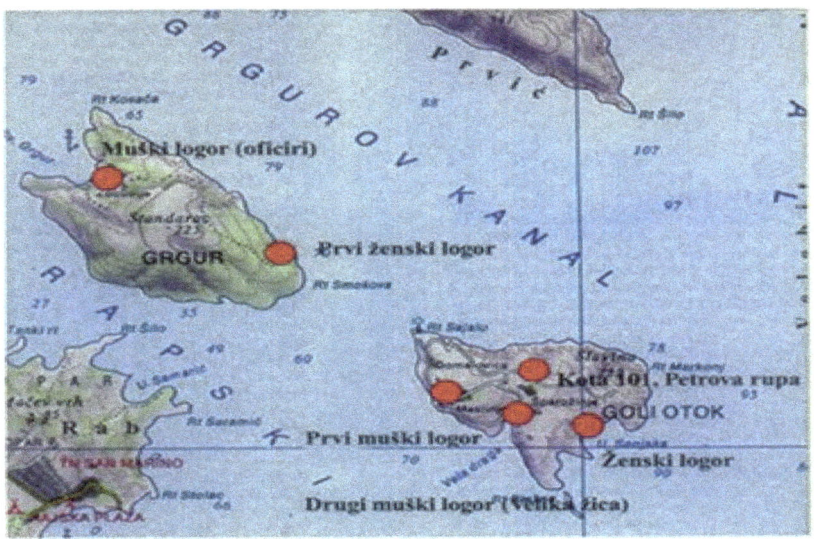

Figure 1 - Bare Island and Grgur (2)

Figure 2 - Meanders of Ćehotine
Author: Željko Vujović

A PSYCHOANALYTIC VIEW OF THE GREAT POLITICAL MOVEMENTS OF THE 20TH CENTURY - FASCISM AND COMMUNISM

– In the chaotic murmur of an unclear destiny –

Elijah is from Podgorica, a "Cikotić who drank water from Ribnica". The story and events from his Microcosm lead him to reflect on the history of the 20th century in the Macrocosm. The story in his Microcosm is not original. It is a consequence, a reflection of the story that was created in the Macrocosm.

Giovanni Gentile (1875-1944, age 68), Benito Mussolini (1883-1945, 62 years old), Adolf Hitler (1889-1945, age 56), Antonio de Oliveira Salazar (1889-1970, 81 years old), Francisco Franco (1892-1975, 83 years old).[4]

Karl Marx (1818-1883, 65 years old), Vladimir Ilyich Lenin (1870-1924, 54 years old), Josip Visarinovich Stalin (1878-1953, 75 years old), Mao Zedong (1893-1976, 83 years old), Josip Boz Tito (1892-1980, 88 dinars)7, Kim Il Sung (1912-1994, 82 years) Fidel Castro (1926-2016, 90 years).[5]

"For me, gods and men are equal, in the chaotic chaos of an unclear fate." Gods and men pass by me, and they are no more to me than they were to those who believed in them. ◊ new saints, saints of new cities, they all walk in the death march (pilgrimage or funeral) of error and illusion. All are marching, and dreams are marching behind them, hollow shadows on the earth, which the worst dreamers believe to be solid ground: sad ideas without form and soul, Freedom, Human

---

4   Creators and implementers of fascism. History condemned them for the evil they inflicted on humanity.

"Tito was very intelligent, cunning, and a real genius of manipulation." He "overwhelmed" two great revolutions, two world wars, several years of imprisonment, and several official marriages."; "Tito - one career, psychobiography of Josip Broz Tito", Source:https://www.youtube.com/watch?v=ncW55 i36G54, (27.12.2022) Dr. Vladimir Adamović "Three dictators: Stalin, Hitler, Tito", Publisher Informatika, Belgrade 2008; Anđelko Cvejić, "Three elections in a dictatorship", Copyright © Politika, 2022

5   Elijah's point of view is: "All the personalities from this group are unoriginal." Mutual imitators. Their deeds (misdeeds especially). They have their origins in the eastern despots (B.R.). King Marx stands out from this group because "before Marx and after Marx everything is not the same", but since "everything flows and everything changes" (Heraclitus), Marx also changes. In addition, whether we like it or not, "The Earth is spinning the same way as before, and the tilt of the Earth's axis has hardly changed."

Happiness, Better Future, and Social Science, drag through the solitude of darkness ◊ in the hands of beggars who ◊ moved into the gardens of the house of defeat." The author of these lines, Fernando Pessoa (1888-1935, 47 years old) was a contemporary of most of the personalities mentioned in the first two paragraphs of this chapter, but he does not mention them, not even his countryman Antonio de Oliveiro Salazar, practically his age, who, in truth, lived thirty-five years longer than him. Perhaps he may be taken to have mentioned it implicitly in the treatise on deplorable ideas. Did Salazar know that Fernando Pessoa existed? In one place, Fernando Pessoa briefly mentioned Lenin as the founder of the state. (12/27/2)

◊

Russians, young people, who are coming to Montenegro these days for who knows what reasons, and one of those reasons is the war in Ukraine, Putin, Lavrov, and their collaborators, they say: "They are criminals!". On the other hand, Vedrana Rudan says: "I don't support Putin, but if I were in his place, I wouldn't allow NATO to get so close to me." All in all, it is difficult and unfair to say that politics is not the oldest profession in the world, and domestic politics and politicians cannot be exempted from that qualification. They are far from original. Bearing in mind their immutability in the last thirty years, the association and thought of Eastern despotisms are inevitable. Let's be broad-minded and put the pressure of totalitarianism out of our minds. There remains the third possibility of a consumer society, which Orwell characterized with the order "you need". We live with this "need" and the popular proverb "craft is gold". Politicians can rub their hands with satisfaction at their craft.

"These hills" are in the same place where they once were. True, some of them, in the vicinity of Podgorica, were uprooted by construction machines. One is to extract stone, the necessary building material, and the other is for the waste storage of those same buildings. Concessions were obtained from the State for the possibility of this mining.

Modern roads, and the highway built by the Chinese (where did the Chinese come from now and how in Montenegro?) lead to Serbia faster and more reliably, with greater consumption of fuel, which is not available or is obtained, and who knows how. On the border with Serbia, ramp. Every passenger, both here and there, should be checked and checked by the state to see if they are correct and if they can cross the border and continue. With Croatia, Bosnia, and Albania, likewise. What drives what? Borders are in the head, not in geography.

After all, is it worth taking a psychoanalytical look at the great social movements of the 20th century, fascism and communism, or is Is it simply a chore?

We all have a diagnosis of a disease, which is kept with the doctor. It is now in the Health Information System database. Will we, and when, get real therapy?

In his book "The Tragedy of Genius", Vladimir Stanojević did not mention any of the protagonists mentioned in the first two paragraphs of this chapter. Does that mean that they didn't have a tragedy or that they weren't geniuses? All that remains is the record of Vladimir Adamović, domestic dictator, was a genius manipulator.

(12/28/202)

◊

The great political movements of the 20th century, fascism and communism, have no psyche. It would be necessary for someone, who is competent, to implant their psyche so that they could observe themselves psychoanalytically, that is, to analyze their psyche, which did not exist until now. Before this incorporation of the psyche, it would be wrong to observe them psychoanalytically.

Society and social movements, in general, have no psyche. This also applies to politics and political movements, especially these two great ones from the 20th century. They have no psyche. If it is accepted that the soul is synonymous with the psyche, it could be said that the mentioned political movements are soulless. That, though leads to dubiousness, because the concept of the soul is linked to the prescientific period, although it is fertilized in some modern disciplines. All in all, there is the following statement: "The concept of the soul remains the subject of many debates and speculations, and its true essence is still not understood." To put it mildly, the concept of the soul is amorphous.

(Communism is often equated with socialism and the two are not the same.)

With all that, someone said that Bernard Russell said that he is against communism, because it is not democratic, but he is also against capitalism because it is exploitative.

◊

What to do? Elijah is registered to go skiing, tomorrow, in Bjelasica. Free transport to the ski resort Kolašin 1600 was organized by TO Podgorica. (22.02.2023.)

◊

I was given a simple question: what motivates the main character to engage in the philosophy of Immanuel Kant? Is it loneliness, thinking about transience, where does the "soul" go, what remains after man...?

The question is simple, as are the supplementary sub-questions, but the answer is very complex.

In the previous chapter, the protagonist touched upon the psychoanalytical point of view on the subject of the great political movements of the 20th century, fascism, and communism. At first sight, impossible and incompatible, the concept of psyche, or soul, was introduced into politics and political movements.

The first obstacle encountered is the question: can psychoanalysis be applied to the consideration of political movements? The answer is yes. Can.

The idea of the unconscious mind, which refers to mental processes outside of an individual's consciousness, but affects his behavior, is applied to political movements by examining the unconscious motives and desires of individuals who participate in these movements. People may be drawn to a political movement as a way to fulfill their unconscious desires and deal with unresolved psychological conflicts. The idea of projection refers to the tendency to attribute one's unconscious desires or traits to others. Individuals within a movement can project their unconscious desires onto the movement as a whole or onto political opponents. The idea of projection refers to the tendency to attribute one's unconscious desires or traits to others. Individuals within a movement can project their unconscious desires onto the movement as a whole or onto political opponents.

For the main character of this story and his motives for dealing with the philosophy of Immanuel Kant is the fact that, at this moment in his life, the concept of the soul and the personal intrapsychic conflicts that arise came to the fore.

He chose not to engage in politics and political movements as an active participant, but that choice did not save him. Politics him by marginalizing him, and at certain moments and stages of his life, to the level of accurate and precise assessment of his best friend, who said: "They want to separate you from your soul".

The main character's motive for dealing with the philosophy of Immanuel Kant is to know his soul and establish peace and harmony with himself.

◊

It has been scientifically proven that a person physically can survive and overcome anything, but the soul, those individual scars?! What have great respected minds said about?

– NON-INSTITUTIONAL CONSIDERATIONS –
KANT IN IGOR CVEJIĆ'S DOCTORAL DISSERTATION

Three basic powers of the soul

The soul is the essence of being. We single out and consider only real beings, independent (substances) and non-independent (accidents). A substance exists even though it is not determined by another thing. An accident does not exist if it is not determined by something else. Substance and accident are correlative terms. An accident cannot be understood without its natural ability to belong to a substance.

Force or power is the ability to act, anything that can produce an effect. Active powers draw strength from substance. The substance contains within itself the source of its changes. The source of change is forced. A force is the relationship between a substance and an accident, if the substance contains the reason for belonging to the accident, that is, only the predicate of the relationship of the substance. Force is not the real reason. The real reason is substance. How many basic forces the soul has is a metaphysical question. It is not a question about the source but about the relations of substance with accidents. So, the soul is not a force, but it has a force. Each substance can have multiple forces because it has multiple relationships. Force (power) is the inner principle of the possibility of action. It is the predisposing reason for the creation of an action.

The three basic powers of the soul are the power of knowledge, the power of desire, and the power of feeling pleasure and displeasure.

Causality model

A cause-and-effect relationship is a relationship between one object, event, or representation with another object, event, or representation, in which one precedes the other, which is the effect, as a cause.

Kant's understanding of causation is interpreted as the exercise of the causal force of relations, the internal reason of which is in some substance, which is therefore called a cause.

The subjective cause of a performance: they are causes to produce themselves, to sustain themselves. It is about the relationship between the performance (mental state, as the first preceding event) and the change in the subject (new mental state, feelings, or maintenance of the performance itself in time, as the second event, which follows) as a consequence.

A representation that produces a desire to maintain its state is called pleasure.

Representations that become causes for the production of objects are called cravings.

Causality leads to the concept of action, action to the concept of force, and force to the concept of substance. Force is the predisposing reason for the reality of an action.

Force is the relationship of substance to inseparably belonging accidents. To us, force is causation.

More power of knowing

Kant believes that the question of the basic powers of the soul has gone beyond empirical observation and has become part of transcendental idealism. The powers of the soul are conditioned by the a priori principles underlying them. Power is derived as the ability to determine accidents based on principles independent of experience (external causes of change). Those principles belong to the "higher" powers of cognition: reason, the power of judgment, and the mind.

These three higher powers of knowledge give the three powers of the soul, which contains, a priori principles; reason for the power of knowledge, the mind for the power of will, and the power of judgment for the feeling of pleasure and displeasure.

Determining reason and a priori principle

A reason is a driver for a decision or action (motive, incentive, cause). In this sense, Kant distinguishes three types of reasons: a) reason of possibility (ratio essendi), b) reason of reality (ratio fiendi), and c) reason of knowledge (ratio cognoscenti). Apart from this division, Kant divides reasons into logical and real. A logical reason has, as IN THE CHAOTIC MURMUR OF AN UNCLEAR DESTINY predicate, a consequence that is identical to it based on the principle of identity, and a real reason has a consequence that is not identical to it, not according to the rule of identity.

The determining reason tells (determines) what the world should be like. The description's reason tells what the world is like, what it was like, or what it will be like.

The a priori principle refers to or denotes reasoning or meaning that comes from theoretical deduction rather than from observation and experience.

Matter and form: isolating the subject of transcendental philosophy

Philosophy is primarily concerned with formal thought. Formal knowledge is the main job of philosophy. It is divided into: - the formal part, which refers only to pure forms of thought, i.e. general logic, and - the material part, which takes into account the objects in question.

Material philosophy does not simply consider the objects of experience, but only insofar as it is possible to know about them mentally according to a priori concepts. That step that distinguishes material philosophy from empirical sciences (or applied philosophy) is possible if transcendental logic deals with forms of thought, not abstracting from the subject, but only if they relate to the subject a priori.

Transcendental aesthetics

Since transcendental philosophy abstracts from the senses, as material content, the question of transcendental aesthetics is a question about pure perceptions, that is, about the forms in which they are given to us. Kant's thesis is that there are two such pure forms: the form of external sense, that is, space, and the form of internal sense, that is, time. External senses are the ability to be affected by external objects through feelings. (Five senses: touch, taste, smell, hearing, and sight). The inner sense is the ability to be affected by our own soul. Basic characteristics of Kant's conception of the inner sense: "[sense] in which the soul shows itself or its inner state", [2] "What a person suffers while affected by the game of his thoughts", [3] "the power of awareness of his existence ". Time is shown as a form of inner sense, ie. observation of ourselves and our inner state. Time always represents the form of an internal sense, not an external one, because it does not express any properties of phenomena, but only their relationship in time. All appearances of an external object are given in space and time, and every internal state is in time.

◊

Awareness is important for several reasons, both on an individual and societal level.

- Personal growth: Awareness of our thoughts, emotions, and behavior can help us identify patterns that may be hindering our personal growth. By understanding ourselves better, we can make positive changes and improve our overall well-being.

- Relationships: Being aware of our own emotions and how they affect others can help us communicate better and build stronger relationships. It can also help us empathize with others and understand their perspectives.

- Decision-making: Awareness allows us to make informed decisions based on a clear understanding of our goals and values. It can help us evaluate options and make choices that are in line with our priorities.

- Personal safety: Awareness of our surroundings and potential dangers can help us stay safe and avoid risks.

- Social issues: More broadly, awareness is key to addressing social issues such as discrimination, inequality, and environmental concerns. Without awareness, these problems can go unnoticed and unresolved.

In short, awareness helps us understand ourselves and the world around us, make better decisions, and improve our relationships and well-being.

Consciousness

Kant distinguishes between two types of consciousness: a) psychological consciousness (conscientia psychologica) - subjective, consists of intuition, "perception directed at ourselves". b) logical consciousness (conscientia logica) - consciousness that should be directed at objects, not ourselves.

The condition of the unity of the idea is the activity of the subject. The traditional fundamental unity of perception, intellectual consciousness is spontaneity, which is also the reason for the unity of empirical self-awareness, emiri apperception, which belongs to the inner sense which is receptivity. Intellectual consciousness is the pure activity of one's thoughts. No perceptual mediation is necessary for pure apperception. Kant summarizes the understanding of consciousness as follows:

1) All ideas do not have the phenomenological property of manifesting as consciousness.

2) Some idea has the manifesting themselves phenomenologically as consciousness if it belongs to the unity of the consciousness of the thinking subject.

3) There is a difference between empirical and intellectual self-consciousness: a) empirical self-consciousness consists in perceiving our state, b) intellectual self-consciousness consists of pure apperception which is object-oriented,

4) The reason for the empirical unity of self-awareness can, in the case of cognition, be found in intellectual self-awareness, that is, in the the fundamental unity of apperception.

The transcendental unity of apperception unites in one concept of the object all the diversity that is given in one perception. If the rules on the synthesis of diversity in one perception of an object are made into concepts, then Kant calls these basic conditions categories, concepts of reason, which refer to the possible synthesis of diversity into objective unity. The reason, that is, the transcendental unity of perception, is the reason for possible knowledge.

The inner sense contains the power of perception itself, but without any variety about it. It does not contain any particular perception which is possible only based on awareness of its determination using the transcendental action of the imagination. Reason does not find a connection of variety in the inner sense, but produces it by affecting this sense. Diversity should be determined in the inner sense, and that determination has its origin in reason. Based on this, reason figures as a (real) determinative reason for the unity of the diversity of the inner sense.

◊

As I write this, I remember Branka. I won't forget her. She is not here. She is not in our apartment. She is not in the apartment where she lived with her mother and brother until she got married. The other day, unprovoked by anything from the outside, some inner urge took me down the paths of my youth and led me to that apartment where she was a virgin. Now her daughter-in-law lives there. Alone. The mother and brother died a long time ago, and the brother's two sons grew up, got married, and have their own families.

Where should I place and how should I describe this pain in the stomach and stomach, which smolders and grows unforgettable? Unforgettable, which opposes and confronts the knowledge that it is not there. In which part of consciousness is it? In the subconscious? In the unconscious part of consciousness? Is it regret because she is not there? Can it be appealed? It's a pain. It needs to be treated. (January 16, 2023)

SOUL, PSYCHE, AND MIND

There is no single, universally accepted definition of the soul. From a scientific perspective, the idea of the soul does not fall within the scope of empirical research, because, in general, it refers to the nonphysical aspect of human existence, which cannot be directly observed or measured by scientific methods. The current situation is such that the nature of the soul is discussed in the fields of philosophy, neuroscience, and psychology. Outside the framework of empirical research, there is a belief that the soul is a unique aspect of each individual and that it carries with it the consciousness, memory, and identity of the person. Additionally, the soul can be seen as a metaphorical representation of one's deepest belief being or essence, which includes emotions values, and spiritual beliefs. In this way, through these concepts, the soul enters the mental content of the personality.

A detailed analysis of the content of footnotes 40 to 47 concludes that the position that the soul is only an idea that refers to the nonphysical an aspect of human existence is very controversial and problematic. On the contrary! Footnotes 40 to 47 indicate that the concept of the soul exists and runs through various, indisputable scientific disciplines and that, with the stated position, scientific research is forcibly reduced, and narrowed down to empirical research.

Psyche is a part of the whole personality. The principle of personality revival. The entire mental world, conscious and unconscious. Constituent parts of the psyche are perception, attention, thinking, emotions, knowledge, memory, and ability.

The mind is the ability (power) of understanding as a whole psychic functioning. It consists of reason and intuition with the affective and conative spheres of personality. The different meanings of the term in the literature are the result of different emphasis on reason, as a part of the mind, that is, the intuitive and affective-conative part. The scientific mind is based more on reason, and the artistic mind is more on the intuitive and affective-conative side of the human mind.

Within the framework of German classical philosophy, the mind is defined as everything that is a priori given to the human spirit, including transcendental categories.

In psychology, the concept of mind is close to the concept of spirit and soul. As such, it participates in the old philosophical problem of the spirit-body relationship within the framework of monism and dualism.

Philosophy is looking for a complete solution to the relationship between mind and body. Psychology does not see the mind (spirit) - body relationship as either completely monistic or dualistic. Most psychological theories are monistic with the predominance of mind or body.

Today's psychiatry has several etiological, therapeutic, and diagnostic approaches, which are also its narrower branches. Biological psychiatry bases its approach on the biological basis of the origin of mental illnesses and psychopharmacological treatment. The approach of social psychiatry is based on studying and changing the process of interpersonal relationships and improving a person's social functioning. Psychotherapy is based on studying and changing intrapsychic processes, and treatment is based on the therapist's psychological influence through verbal and emotional communication. Child and adolescent psychiatry deals with the treatment of psychological problems of children and youth, alcoholology with the treatment of alcoholism, and addictions, and liaison (collaborative) psychiatry by treating psychological problems that occur with physical illnesses. Forensic or court psychiatry is defined as the application of psychiatry for judicial purposes, and it deals with psychiatric expertise.

Psychoanalysis is a method for the diagnosis and treatment of various psychological problems. This type of analysis focuses on the unconscious mind. It is more thorough than, for example, behavioral therapy, so it may take longer for the patient to notice improvement. The founder of this type of analysis as it is known today is Sigmund Freud. The Austrian researcher is known for his controversial theories and ideas and is often at the center of discussions. At the core of this theory is Freud's belief that all people have unconscious thoughts, desires, and feelings. It helps people deal with this emotional baggage. The focus of these types of sessions is on free conversation about experiences and feelings. It is a psychotherapeutic method, just like behavioral therapy or cognitive behavioral therapy. The difference between the two is that psychoanalysis can go deeper into traumatic issues. Psychoanalysis requires significantly more time and sessions to achieve noticeable

Id, Ego and Superego

Sigmund Freud's most famous work deals with the human psyche. He believed that the psyche consisted of more than one aspect. He structured the psyche into the ID, EGO, and SUPEREGO. Each of these structural elements develops at different stages of life. These three aspects should not be confused with parts or other physical objects. According to Freud, the ID is a primitive and instinctive part of the brain. This part is responsible for storing sexual and aggressive drives and hidden memories. The SUPEREGO acts as a moral compass, and the EGO is the realistic part that mediates between the desires of the ID and the SUPEREGO.

Figure 3 - "Man is man's greatest secret"[6]

---

6   Petar II Petrović Njegoš, "Light of microcosm", Rad, Belgrade 1990

◊

Many claimed that "suffering is a sublime feeling". I guarantee it's excruciating, anxious, sometimes expected, and sometimes unfairly inflicted. Beware of:

LOCAL GODS AND PEOPLE'S GOVERNMENT

The delusions of childhood are mostly based on rewards for good behavior and punishments for bad behavior. Half of the world is made up of "true believers" (about a billion Christians and half a billion Muslims), for whom the rules related to eternal life are the most important. The "heathen" half of the world is judged by the local gods and the people's government during their lifetime. A child rarely leaves his illusions. Some misconceptions are universal because their origin is related to the first months of life, and maybe even the womb itself. They create a magical world, which man will visit later, only through love, sex, or drugs (or in the case of evil people, through massacre). At best, parental guidance reads: "Do good and nothing bad can happen to you", a motto that forms the basis of the ethical systems of all countries throughout written history. At worst, it reads "The world would be much better if some people didn't live on it and if you kill them, you will gain omnipotence and inaccessibility."

◊

While the new, modern Man called Uve is facing himself, time is running. Maybe some things are predestined, and some things happen to us because we don't know them enough.

THE SCENARIO OF LIFE

Transactional analysis is a branch of social psychiatry[7], game analysis is a special side of transactional analysis. Social communication is based on three types of hunger: hunger for stimulation, hunger for recognition, and hunger for structure. It has been noted that the most preferred forms of teasing are those provided by physical closeness. Experiments have shown that the absence of sugar can cause a severe mental illness in a transient form or a temporary mental disorder. The hunger for stimulation, for the biological survival of the organism, has the same value as the hunger for food. When the period of physical closeness with the mother is over, a man's entire life remains a dilemma on which his fate and even his survival depend. On one side are all those social, psychological, and biological forces that stand in the way of maintaining physical closeness in the style of a small baby, and on the other is the insatiable desire for just such closeness. In most life situations, a person is forced to compromise, called sublimated feelings[8]. Irritation not only has a positive effect on the physical, mental, and emotional development of the individual but also the biochemical composition of the brain. By increasing the complexity of the compromise, everyone becomes more and more unique in their search for recognition. It is precisely these differences that bring diversity to social communication and determine the destiny of an individual. The eternal torment of the human being is how to structure the hours of life that he spends in Java.

To satisfy the three primary types of hunger, man structures his time, according to the degree of complexity, into rituals, pastimes,

---

7   Socijalna psihijatrija je grana psihijatrije koja se fokusira na odnos između društvenih faktora i mentalnog zdravlja. Ispituje kako društveni faktori, kao što su kultura, rasa, etnička pripadnost, društvana klasa, struktura porodice i zajednica, utiču na razvoj i liječenje poremećaja mentalnog zdravlja. Socijalna psihijatrija istražuje kako društvene intervencije, kao što su programi mentalnog zdravlja u zajednici, mogu da poboljšaju is- hode mentalnog zdravlja. Socijalna psihijatrija je interdisciplinarna. Oslanja se na polja kao što su sociologija, antropologija, psihologija i javno zdravlje. Bavi se razumjevanjem društvenog konteksta u kojem nastaju poremećaji mentalnog zdravlja i razvojem i razvojem intervencija koje se bave individualnim i društvenim faktorima mentalnog zdravlja.

8   Sublimirana osjećanja se odnose na emocije ili impulse koji su preusmjereni ili potisnuti do tačke u kojoj ih pojedinac više ne percipira svjesno, ali i dalje postoje na nesvjesnom nivou. Ova osjećanja mogu da se smatraju „sublimiranim" jer su transformisana ili uzdignuta u društveno prihvatljivije izlaze. Posmatra se kao pozitivna adaptacija. Omogućava pojedincima da izraze svoje emocije na produktivniji i konstruktivniji način, umjesto da djeluju na njih napotencionalno štetan način.

games, closeness, and action. A ritual is an ordinary series of simple complementary transactions, programmed by social forces beyond the individuals involved. Pastimes are activities that people engage in for pleasure and enjoyment during their free time. The main goal of leisure is to structure certain time intervals. The beginning and end of that interval are usually announced by some skill or ritual. They are programmed elastically so that each of the participants achieves the maximum gain or advantage during that interval. The better it is adapted, the more leisure it will have. Games are a series of complementary, hidden transactions, converging towards a very specific, predictable outcome. On the surface, it is visible that it is a set of transactions that are renewed, often in an identical way, with apparent credibility behind which the real motivation is hidden. It is a series of moves that hide a trap or "stunt". Games are clearly distinguished from rituals, pastimes, closeness, and work (action) by two main characteristics: in them, one is fooling around and someone always shines. Games are, by definition, unfair, and their relationship is not only exciting but also dramatic. Intimacy is the only fully satisfying answer to the hunger for stimulation, the hunger for recognition, and the hunger for structure. Her act is the prototype of love fulfillment. Work (doing) is the simplest, most suitable, and most useful method of structuring time. It is a processing project that provides us with the external world.

EGO-STATES are psychological realities. EGO is the experience and perception of one's self. EGO-STATE is a coordinated system of feelings and a set of forms of behavior. PARENT is an ego-state that resembles parental figures (extrapsychic). ADULT is an ego–state that is autonomously focused on objective reality (non-psychic). A CHILD is an ego–state that represents archaic remains, i.e. still active ego-states in early childhood (archaepsychic). A CHILD is many times the most valuable part of a person. It can give a person's life what a real child brings to family life: irresistibility, pleasure, and creativity. A child has intuition, creativity, and the drive for spontaneity and enjoyment. ADULT is necessary to survive.

It processes data and probabilities of various combinations and possibilities, which is essential for successfully dealing with the outside world. A PARENT has two main functions. It enables a man to be successful as a real parent to his children. The team promotes the survival of the human species. It automates many reactions. In this way, it saves a person's time and energy.

A transaction is a unit of social relationships. When two or more people get together, sooner or later one of them will speak or show in some other way that they are "noticing" the presence of the others. This is called transactional charm. Someone else will then say or do something related to that charm. This is called a transactional response. The transactional analysis determines which ego state threw out the transactional charm, and which responded with a transactional response. Transactions can be complementary, hidden, and corner. Complementary transactions take place under the natural order and healthy human relations. Hidden transactions activate more than two ego states simultaneously. Games are based on such transactions. Corner transactions are those in which three ego states are activated.

Games are created by raising a child, an educational process in which the child learns which games to play and how to perform them. His knowledge and mastery of skills, rituals, and pastimes determine what opportunities will be available to him under normal circumstances. The games he plays determine how he will use those opportunities and what, for him, will result from those situations for which he qualified. The essence of the game is its climax or gain, but they are always planned in such a way that, along the road, they provide the greatest pleasure in every phase of the game. Games fit into the unconscious life plan or "scenario" of every person and represent its driving part. They serve a person to fill the time while waiting for the final life achievement, i.e. while gradually advancing on it from various directions at the same time.

A good game is one whose social contribution outweighs the complexity of its motives, especially if the player is clean with those motives, without feelings of futility or cynicism. A good game contributes both to the well-being of the player and the development of the player. Examples of good games are: action player, cavalier, happy to help, local wise man, they will be glad they knew me.

Personal autonomy is achieved by freeing oneself from parental influences. This is not at all easy because they are deeply rooted and represent the necessity of biological and social survival during the first two or three decades of life. Achieving autonomy consists in overthrowing all those nonsenses that rule man. That overthrow is never final. Man is forced to constantly fight against falling into old patterns.

First, it needs to remove the burden of the entire polemic or family historical tradition. It should overturn the influence of individual parents and social and cultural backgrounds. He needs to obtain a "divorce by agreement" from his parents so that, occasionally and by agreement, he can visit them, but without further recognition of their power.[9]

---

9   **Source:** [18][19] Licenca: *CC BY 4.0*

TODOR BAKOVIĆ AND FERNANDO PESOA

TODOR BAKOVIĆ: The depression of Montenegrins comes from Christianity, and the optimism comes from the cult of the mother.

FERNANDO PESOA: When like the day that dawns after a stormy night, Christianity passed over souls, the damage it imperceptibly caused them was visible, but all the destruction it caused will be seen only when it is completely over.

KARL MARX (1818–1883, 64 years old): Christmas is a bourgeois conspiracy to oppress the proletariat.

EMANUEL KANT (1724 - 1804, 79 years old): You must have a Merry Christmas!

ADAM SMITH (1723 - 1790, 69 years old): An invisible hand will determine whether Christmas is happy.

RENE DESCARTES (1596 – 1650, 53 years old): I think it's Christmas so I'm happy.

ARISTOTLE (384 B.H. – 322 B.H., 61–62 years): What is Christmas?

Elijah observed that, as a neuropsychiatrist, Todor Baković, using scientific methods concluded that Montenegrins have a depressive character, which they acquired through the doctrine of Christianity. Christianity teaches man that they are suffering, tormented, and suffering of sublime feelings to which man is condemned, as is the case with Jesus Christ.

On the other hand, medicine has clearly and indisputably classified depression as a disease that should and can be treated.

Based on the model of causation and the relationship between cause and effect, Elijah concludes that Montenegrins should reject Christianity and thus contribute to the healing of their depression.

Elijah found additional support for this opinion and position with Fernando Pessoa, who stated that Christianity, imperceptibly, caused damage and destruction to the entire humanity. Damage and destruction will be seen and understood only when Christianity is completely gone.

In addition, Elijah cites an excerpt from a lecture given by Bertrand Russell on March 6, 1927, at Battersea Town Hall, sponsored by the South London Chapter of the National Secular Society.

"Why I am not a Christian." What should we do?

"We need to stand on our own two feet and look the world in the face - its good and bad sides, its beauty, its ugliness; to see the world as it is and not be afraid of it. The world should be conquered with intelligence, and not just sit in it in slavish submission to your fear.

The whole idea of God came from ancient Eastern despotisms.

It is an idea that is not worthy of a free man.

When you hear people in church putting themselves down and talking about themselves as wretched sinners and all, it's despicable and unworthy of a self-respecting human being. We need to stand up and look the world openly in the face. We should do everything we can, and that will always be better than what these others have done all these ages.

A good world requires knowledge, kindness, and courage; it is not necessary to yearn regretfully for the past and hinder our intelligence with words uttered long ago by ignorant people. A fearless view of the world and free intelligence are needed. We need hope for the future, not looking back on the past, which is dead and will be far surpassed by the future, which will be created by our mind."

Elijah joins Bertrand Russell, and Fernando Pessoa completely, and Todor Baković in treating the depression of Montenegrins, by neutralizing and eliminating the damage and destruction that Christianity has caused them.

In addition, medicines of scientific medicine for the treatment of depression, Todor Baković will prescribe without Elijah.

Are you aware that, in addition to what we see, there is also "what we do not see"? Sometimes that has more of an impact than what we perceive. How do we get to know him? Let's go, guys! Follow me!

AT THE INTERSECTION WITH TRAFFIC LIGHTS ON POBREŽJE

Hotel "Union". Fully glazed hotel lobby. A table in the corner, right next to the intersection. The front high glass wall and a zebra crosswalk are separated by a narrow sidewalk one meter wide. It's raining outside. It's pouring. Cars pass each other, guided by traffic lights. Along King Nikola Street, towards Pobrežje and Zabjelo, and in the opposite direction, towards Sat-tower. Others come from Srdjan Aleksić Boulevard, cross into Montenegrin Serdar Street, and continue past Čepurak, Union Bridge, the American Embassy, and beyond. Opposite them, in the same direction, cars come, which, having crossed the traffic lights, come to the next intersection with traffic lights, from which the fork of the roads straight, towards the bus station, left, towards the city center and right, towards Skadar Lake and the Adriatic Sea. Three hundred meters from the intersection, King Nikola Street, which was formerly called Petar Matović Street, at the front end of the ground floor residential building, second in line, there is an apartment, the legacy of Elijah's late grandfather, mother's father. He got the apartment from the Municipality, once upon a time, long ago, after that war, because he worked as an official in the Municipality. Now, in that apartment, lives a daughter-in-law, Elijah's aunt, the widow of her late uncle, Elijah's peer, who died recently, in the middle of February this year. The other descendants of Elijah's grandfather moved away a long, long time ago. In Sarajevo, Belgrade... It could be said that they never even lived in that apartment, but they came regularly, every year, while their parents were alive. Two of the "moved away" sons returned. One, in the mid-seventies of the last century, from Paraćin, Serbia, where he worked with his wife in a fabric factory after graduating from the Faculty of Law in Belgrade. He died ten years ago. He had his apartment in Brotherhood Unity Street. He has his descendants. The other returned, and escaped from Sarajevo, during the war years of the 1990s. He has his apartment, on the top floor of a block of flats, on Bracan Bracanović Street. And he has his descendants. Elijah's house, that is, a third of the house, that came to him from the inheritance, the marital property of his father and mother, is from the place where he is sitting now. Five hundred meters from this intersection, in the second row of houses, in the middle. Half of that street is also called Kings Nikola Street, and the other half is Ljubović Street. To the left of the intersection, behind tall pine trees and a small settlement with low houses, now, so to speak, shantytowns, which have existed there since Elijah can remember, is the beloved, never forgotten, the most beautiful, the best in the world Elementary School "Milorad Musa Burzan". Strict teacher Tomaš Marković made the first roll call for Elijah, the student of the champion. Good and very good teacher Slavka Kadović, in the second, third, and fourth grades. Teacher Vaso Raičković, class leader in the fifth grade. In the sixth, seventh, and eighth grades, the class leader, the unforgettable, stunning, classy Sonja Žižić. Teachers Lazar Babović, Slobodan Simović, Slavko Vukčević, Mojsije Ivanović, Branko Dubak... teachers of physical and health education, (school championship in football, assembling the School's representation and competition with representatives of other primary schools in the city, drama section, choir...).

The rain is pouring, pouring, everywhere on the asphalt. Cars pass by constantly. A girl with a red umbrella crosses the pedestrian crossing. A man, across the street, under a pine tree, has opened a black umbrella and is standing. Another girl, in a dark blue raincoat with a hood and a blue umbrella, crosses the pedestrian crossing and continues on the sidewalk towards Pobrežje. Time has stopped. The man with the black umbrella moved, turned and left along Srđan Aleksić Boulevard, towards „Gintash".

„Gintash" - what a name!? New, and foreign, but it has already become recognizable. It has become homely. Across the street from the beloved elementary school. The left part of „Gintash", towards The Beautiful Kata Building is a new, modern green market. Upstairs, on the first floor, is a beautifully decorated flea market with "nothing missing". In the same large building called „Gintash", in a special corner, on the right and the first floor, is the Ramada Hotel. The front of the building is called the „Mall of Montenegro". Mall of Montenegro - what is it? Shopping mall in Podgorica. What are those words? Known. Every day, but what do they mean? Mall? Elijah remembers he was in America, in Florida. There, for the first time, he saw and read that word. It searches Google Translate to find the meaning. Mall - shopping center, promenade, alley. America came, and moved to his elementary school! Shopping - shopping, shopping. There are no more markets, bazaars, and market days, like in the past when the Nuse came from Malaysia, in their colorful costumes, woven on looms. Now it can be bought, sold, and traded every day. Except for Sundays. Think, the Mall is closed, and locked on Sundays. Only the big inscription on the front wall „Mall of Montenegro" remains.

Does anyone remember that, once upon a time, in the place where „Gintash" is now and the residential block behind it, towards the Bus station, all the way to the Railway station, there was a desolate field, a part of the wide Ćemovsko field? Physical education and health education teachers emphasized Miko Bracović, practically from the beginning of the school year, had special classes in that field. All students had mandatory sports equipment: shorts, a T-shirt and sneakers. They practiced landing exercises. They were preparing for the landing on Youth Day, the twenty-fifth of May. They performed their "small" landing at the Stadium „Future", below Gorica hill. Elijah remembers how satisfied and happy he was, on the grass field of the Stadium, together with a harmoniously arranged crowd of students from other schools, when he performed a handstand, and another student-trainer held his legs at the ankles, so that they were completely straightened, raised in height. It was wonderful on a bright May day.

The main, big landing was in Belgrade, at the JNA stadium. Those who were not at the Stadium JNA could watch that landing on television. Ismeta Krvavac sang the lyrics of the song "I see the fields that are golden with grain and on the hill, I see my native home. Every moment I think of you, my land"

The rain has almost stopped falling. Here, a new City Traffic bus, „Capital Podgorica", passes through the intersection. Transportation by buses of the City Transport Company used to be the main transportation through the city and to all suburban areas. At one point he stopped. Gone. It was gone for a long time. Taxis appeared. In large numbers. There are even now. A lot. How everything changes! "Everything flows, everything changes" – said Heraklit. "You can't step in, step foot, in the same place, in the same river twice!" Yes, yes, that's what the teacher Branko Dubak told to the pupils in elementary school, in one of the physics classes, that Heraclitus said that too.

The rain stopped completely.

CONTROL EXAMINATION WITH A SPECIALIST DOCTOR

– In the chaotic murmur of an unclear destiny –

On 30.08.2022. Elijah of Th under received a referral for a checkup with a specialist urologist. The instruction is valid for six months. The date of the inspection is 11.11.2022. He must wait almost two and a half months to have that control examination. It seems to him that it is a long time. He remembers that he had a previous check-up for the same diagnosis at the „Codra" Clinic in September 2020 and the doctor told him to come for a check-up regularly, every six months. He was referred to the "Codra" Clinic by his chosen doctor from the Health Center. He didn't have to wait long then. The review was done, so to speak, within three days. Now he can't do that anymore. "Codra" is closed. It was reported in the media that they "inflated the invoices" and that, because of this, they can no longer work. What to do? Two years have passed since that last inspection in "Codra". Elijah failed to make a control examination immediately after six months. Is it his fault? Negligence? With the new instructions from the chosen doctor, he got an appointment for a follow-up examination after two years and two months. He feels panic, and pressure to do something, not to wait, to finish the examination before the scheduled appointment. He went to the urology clinic at the KBC Polyclinic. He is talking to the nurse, who is sitting at the counter. He shows her the directions and says that he would like to be examined because, a long time ago, the six-month period for the control examination expired, and the instruction stated that he should wait two months for the examination appointment. The nurse refers him to the Emergency Center, on the ground floor, so that they can write him a referral for an examination there. Go to the Emergency Center. Medical The nurse at the desk in the Emergency Center tells him that they do not give instructions, to return to the Urology Outpatient Clinic. They can review it if they want. He goes again to the Urology clinic. The nurse tells him to go to his Chosen Doctor so that he can write on the prescription that the examination is urgent. After that, he should come and be examined. He goes to the Health Center with the Chosen Doctor. He tells the nurse at the main desk why he came and that he needs to talk to the Chosen Doctor. The nurse tells him that the Chosen Doctor can't see him and that the Chosen Doctor would tell him everything she told him. At that moment he remembered he did not even see the Chosen

Doctor on 30.08.2022. year, but the nurse at the main desk gave him instructions based on the data recorded on the computer. Point! There is no specialist examination until the scheduled appointment. On 11.11.2022. at the exact scheduled time, at 11:00 a.m., Elijah reported to the nurse at the desk of the Urology Clinic at the KBC Polyclinic.

Nurse: You are not insured. You need to pay a co-payment of eight euros to be examined.

Elijah: How am I not insured?! Here is your health card! Here's a guide from the Chosen Doctor! I waited two months and came exactly at the appointed time!

Nurse: With us, you are treated as if you are not insured.

Elijah suppresses anger and rage: No! You will examine me, and I will, after the examination, refund you those eight euros, if something is wrong. Please understand, that you are a humanist, and medical worker, I have been waiting for this examination for two months and I came at the exact scheduled time.

The nurse is silent. It is being reconsidered: Go to the Health Fund and they will give you a certificate that you are health insured, then come with that certificate and you will be examined. It won't be late.

Elijah goes to the Health Care Fund. He scored, exactly, during the break. He had to wait for the break to end. After a break, he received the requested confirmation. "Insured" again came to the Urology Clinic. The nurse accepted the certificate and the urologist specialist examined him. He took an anamnesis and clinical findings, stated that there were no laboratory and X-ray results, and gave advice, prevention, and prophylaxis. Control of the urologist with the required findings without specifying the date when the control should be performed and how to obtain the required findings. In the instructions of the Chosen Doctor, it was stated that the Chosen Doctor authorizes the specialist urologist to give instructions for all necessary tests. The urologist did not assume that authority. Elijah, with the specialist's report, went to the Chosen Doctor. Prescribed creams are not available in pharmacies. It is not registered with an import permit. The selected doctor prescribed a specialist examination at Old Airport, without specifying the date when the examination should be performed. They can do it if they want to. In the Health Center at Old Airport, the nurse at the main desk returned Elijah, with the mentioned in the Chosen Doctor, so that he could make an appointment for him. In addition, she also gave him the phone number of the Patient Rights Defender to complain if he thinks he has been denied a right. Elijah spoke with the Protector of Patients' Rights. The appointment of the examination is now centrally scheduled, the Protector of Patients' Rights explained to him. Appointments are released from the first to the fifth of the month. What should he do, he asked the Chosen Doctor. "Come then, so you don't miss the appointment," was the answer. He came on the first of December. The chosen doctor was absent, from professional training. On December 2nd, he received an appointment with the Chosen Doctor and received an appointment: on January 31, 2023. Elijah rolled his eyes. To wait two months again! Will these findings be valid for a urologist specialist, obtained after such a long time since they were requested? "I don't know of a service in the Public Health Service where the mentioned examinations and findings can be done in a shorter time" says the chosen Doctor. The magnetic resonance examination is expected for at least three months. Elijah regretfully left the infirmary. He visited all known private polyclinics in the city. Examinations and findings requested by the urologist specialist can be performed without waiting. Price: X-ray – EHO – 26€, PSA – prostate hormone 20€. Will the Chosen Doctor and urologist specialist accept findings from private polyclinics? Private healthcare institutions do not belong to the system of public healthcare institutions.

FINAL DIAGNOSIS: Findings are in order. The patient died. No, no, no! He survived! He can still be super satisfied. All this is much better than in Serbia. Therefore, an examination by a state doctor takes three months, and examinations and findings in private institutions cost 100€ each. The length of waiting for an analogous examination by a state doctor in Croatia, insufficient precise, was estimated at six months. The price of an examination at an accredited private doctor in Croatia cannot be discerned in the chaos of advertisements, which are used to advertise themselves on the Internet, as well as due to the many discount actions they offer. Certainly, they do not cause problems and differences between kuna and euro during billing.

"A stone against a pot or a pot against a stone, the pot will perish."

The System against Elijah or Elijah against the System, Elijah will suffer. No matter how you twist and turn, his destiny.

THE TWELVE DUKE

Good evening Željko. I have read your hopefully working version of the book. I can't tell what genre it belongs to. For now, this is a kind of travelogue. I like it. It is full of emotions but incomplete! You know that a book is like a child. You write it, let it grow a little, and then see what you need to feel, see and write. Kosovi Lug are the villages: Bgovine, Jastreb, Mamućevina, Kosić, Pitoma Loza, Lazine, Strahinjići, Sladojevo Kopito, Šume Bećirovića, Tomaševići, and maybe another village. We are from Begovin, i.e. Milo is from Begovin, but he separated from the family community when he came from Argentina and bought our property in Mamucevina. Zorka, Mileva, Boško and Jovo was born in Begovine, and I, Ranko and Milenko, were born in Mamućevina. Well, now you know something about the Đurovićs, and you should know that those Đurovićs, that is, the Vojvodićs, are the surnames of a number of our relatives, especially for the reason that our house had 12 voivodes. When I finish my memoirs, which I write from time to time and are close to completion, you will receive a memory of Mother Mileva and our family. You should always mention Đurović with pride. Twelve dukes, and among the most intellectuals in Montenegro. Just mentioning Ratko Đurović, a Montenegrin and Yugoslav film screenwriter and cultural historian, one of the first professors at the Dramaturgy Group of the Faculty of Dramatic Arts in Belgrade, would be enough.

◊

I reread this manuscript of yours. He is chaotic noisy and unclear. I think and I am sure that you are in such a state that it is not time to write a book. But it is, to make theses from this manuscript, which will help you to write a serious book in at least one year. The book is written sensibly. You will often change the text, adapting it to the times. Memories of youthful days, dating, weddings, the birth of your beautiful children, and other beautiful, but also sad moments. Systematize them so that they are what they are: one life, which is always short from the aspect of transience. The memories that you describe and mention with longing, grow in your memories, and those of your children and grandchildren, translated into a book that you will write, something that will live in them and remind them of all that is beautiful! Brana Crnčević described it beautifully in one of his songs: "Where are my falconry ancestors, weren't they there, were they dreams?" And ended with the line: "We all owe it to ourselves, to our children, let's be descendants to be ancestors". From one of your wonderful, joint lives filled with happiness and love, to wonderful and successful children, each book will be a wonderful reminder of your ancestors, and even more of your descendants. Best regards, Žarko (January 9, 2023)

◊

I'm flipping through albums with old pictures, memories, memories. I write something down on sheets of paper. It's like I'm reliving something that has passed. I am overcome by a certain sadness, a thought. The uses for a possible book? Afterward, I tear up all those pieces of paper and throw them in the basket. I would like you to find or to find a thread, of interesting theses, which could be significant for the book. Are there any details, or interesting theses of general importance, that you noticed and which should be highlighted and emphasized? Significant to the wider community? What did those dukes, whom you point out, do and have done? Are they all from the same "generation", so they "talk constantly to their generation for centuries"? Who are they an example of? Is there anyone, from the heirs of those famous 12 dukes, who succeeded, following them, to overcome and surpass them nowadays? Are there any of their descendants who reached an important general social position, even if it was a private cafe owner or head waiter in one of the modern tycoon hotels, of which there are incomparably more than 12, as many as there were those distinguished, famous dukes? Why is it written on the Internet that Kosić and Kosovi Lug are the same? Greetings, Željko. (09.01.2023)

SCIENTIFIC WORK

Last spring I started writing a scientific article with the working title "Study of numerical solution of initial boundary value problems involving Maxwell's equations in isotropic media". I thought deeply about how deeply I had forgotten the concept and essence of Maxwell's equations, including Faraday's and Ampere's laws individually.

The summer death sent Maxwell's equations Faraday's law and Ampere's law and many other laws to hell.

I received information from Research Gate about the increase in the number of readers and the increase in citations for my article "Classification Model Evaluation Metrics". The article was published in July 2021 in the International Journal of Advanced Computer Science and Applications Volume 12 (Issue 6):599-606, DOI: 10.14569/ IJACSA. 2021.0120670. I see that, up to this point, it has been read by 5,538 readers, cited by 61 researchers, received one recommendation, and has a high research interest score of 127,.4. It is a score that is far from unstated and unremarkable.

In addition, my article "Gradient Magnetic Field Of MR Scanners", in a reference scientific journal, received, from an anonymous reviewer from Canada, a review that impressed me. Here's what that review says:

"Comments for the author:

First, congratulations to the author for the acceptance of his study on "GRADIENT MAGNETIC FIELD OF MR SCANNER." The manuscript is very precise, and reliable and reveals the key concepts of this study. However, I would like to reveal a few points.

Thank you for assigning me to review this manuscript.

The paper titled "Gradient Magnetic Field of MR Scanner" was a cross-sectional review that explored the knowledge of magnets used to create different magnetic fields. The main superconductor magnets should be made using a cryostat, with cooling vessels with liquid helium and liquid nitrogen, thermal insulation, and other protective elements of the magnetic system.

In this study, the magnets used by the author that exist in basic configurations of MR scanners are analyzed. The scanners are placed in the form of a closed cylindrical cavity that creates its own magnetic fields by passing current through a solenoid, which is maintained at the temperature of a superconductor. This research shows to achieve superconductivity of the material, which creates the main magnetic field, it uses a crystal, with cooling vessels for liquid helium, thermal insulation, and other elements to protect the main magnetic system.

I would like to thank the author for his keen observation and detailed description of the complex structure of the MR scanner magnet and how the resonant frequency changes in a controlled manner at each point of the magnetic field. Evidence shows that microbial fibers of one of the superconductors, NiTi, Nb3Sn, Va3Ga, or MgB2, have been inserted into the copper conductors. It supports and protects winding alloys from damage, ensures mechanical strength, and prevents deformation and vibrations.

In this paper, input-output senses are generated directly by different input-output devices and characterized by appropriate characteristic parameters, and characters (symbols that represent information and the representation of such symbols in a form that can be accepted by a computer) can be generated using visual, auditory, linguistic, mobile and other sensory devices and categorize them according to one or more parameters.

• The table of self-perceptions, as well as the pictures, had much more impact on the manuscript.

• The study has a clear introduction and the explanation is relevant.

• This study, however, highlighted specific misconceptions as an important source that room temperature superconductors, although discovered, are not in the research field of the world's leading laboratories, as possible materials for making magnets for MR scanners.

• Introduction and discussion sections provide useful information for readers. The overall level of work is good. It is an informative study and should be considered for publication.

Journal editors: As this is a high-quality manuscript, it should be published and made available to all readers and researchers.

Work rating:

1. The title is catchy

2. The manuscript provides enough background information for readers in the immediate area to understand the problem/hypotheses

3. The text is well arranged

4. There are no grammatical errors in this article

5. References provided are relevant to the content and accurate

6. There is a more acceptable level of similarity

Comments for the editor:

It can be accepted for publication without any changes.

Work results: Relevance - 9, Originality - 9, Significance - 9, Technical Correctness - 8, Clarity of Presentation/Language - 10."

I expect that the article will be published in the next issue of the magazine "Technique" of the Association of Engineers and Technicians of Serb.

UDC: 621.3.013.2 : 004.352.4.083.3

GRADIENT MAGNETIC FIELD OF MR SCANNERS
Željko Đ. Vujović

Abstract: *The topic of this paper is parts of modern MR devices, in which the magnet windings are located. MR scanner magnets are made of four types of electromagnetic windings: 1) The main magnet, made of superconducting material, creates a variable magnetic field; 2) X coil, made of resistive material, creates a variable magnetic field, horizontally, from left to right, across scanning tube; 3) Y coil creates a varying magnetic field, vertically, from bottom to top; 4) Z coil creates a varying magnetic field, longitudinally, from head to toe, within scanning tube. Superconductors, which create the main magnetic field, should be cooled by liquid helium and liquid nitrogen. Main magnets made of superconductors should use cryostat, with cooling vessels with liquid helium and liquid nitrogen, thermal insulation, and other protective elements of the magnet system. The types of magnets that exist in the basic configurations of MR scanners are analyzed. Scanners in the form of a closed cylindrical cavity create their own, magnetic, fields by passing a current through the solenoid, which is held at the temperature of the superconductor. The superconductors used exclusively are niobium-titanium (NbTi), niobium-tin (Nb_3Sn), vanadium-gallium (V_3Ga), and magnesium-diboride (MgB_2). Only magnesium diboride is a high-temperature superconductor, with a critical temperature of $T_c = 39^0K$. The three remaining superconductors are low temperatures. New high-temperature superconductors have been discovered, as well as room-temperature superconductors. Newly discovered superconducting materials are not used in MR scanners. The magnet structure of the MR scanner is complex. The resonant frequency changes at each point of the field in a controlled manner. The windings of the main magnet made of superconducting material in the form of microbial fibers are built into the copper core. The nonlinear gradient field is created by windings of conductive material. It is added to the main magnetic field. Thus, the resulting magnetic field is obtained.*

Keywords: *nonlinear gradient field, main magnetic field, closed cylindrical cavity create, variable magnetic field, magnetic field, main magnet, high-temperature superconductor*

Paper's File Name: MCA-23-19588#

Journal Title: Modern Chemistry and Applications

Paper Title: GRADIENT MAGNETIC FIELD OF MR SCANNERS

Comment to the author:

Firstly, Congratulations to the author for acceptance of his study on "GRADIENT MAGNETIC FIELD OF MR SCANNERS." The manuscript is very precise and reliable, revealing this study's key concepts. However, I would like to disclose a few points. Thank you for assigning me to review this manuscript. The paper entitled "Gradient Magnetic Field of MR Scanners" was a cross-sectional survey exploring the knowledge of Magnets used to create different magnetic fields. Main magnets made of superconductors should be made of use cryostat, with cooling vessels with liquid helium and liquid nitrogen, thermal insulation, and other protective elements of the magnet system. In this study magnets used by an author that exist in the basic configurations of MR scanners are analyzed. Scanners are placed in the form of a closed cylindrical cavity which creates their own, magnetic, fields by passing a current through the solenoid, which is held at the temperature of the superconductor. This study found that the knowledge to achieve the superconductivity of the material, which creates the main magnetic field, a crystal is used, with cooling vessels for liquid helium, thermal insulation, and other elements to protect the main magnet system. I appreciate the author's keen observation and detailed description of the complex structure of the MR scanner magnet and how the resonant frequency changes in a controlled manner at each point of the magnetic field. Evidence shows that the microbial fibers of one of the superconductors, NiTi, Nb3Sn, Va3Ga, or MgB2, are inserted into the copper conductors. Supports and protects alloy windings from damage provides mechanical strength and prevents deformations and vibrations. In this paper, the input-output senses are generated directly by various input-output devices and characterized by their corresponding characteristic parameters, and characters can be generated by visual sense, auditory sense, language, movement, and other sensory devices and categorized by one or more parameters.

- The tabular representation of the self-perceptions and the figures added much more impact to the manuscript.
- The study has a clear introduction and the explanation is relevant.
- This study however highlighted specific misconceptions as an important source that room-temperature superconductors, although discovered, are not in the field of research of the world's leading laboratories, as possible materials for making magnets for MR scanners.
- The introduction and discussion sections provide useful information for the readers. The overall level of the paper is good. It is an informal study and should be considered for publication.

Journal editors: As this is a high-quality manuscript, should be published and available to all the readers and researchers

Evaluation of Paper
1. The title is attractive
2. The manuscript provides sufficient background information for readers in the immediate field to understand the problem/hypothesis
3. The text is well arranged
4. There are no grammatical errors in this article
5. The references cited are relevant to the content and accurate
6. There is a more acceptable level of similarities

Comment to Editor

It can be Accepted for publication without any changes.

Paper score

Ten-point system	Relevance	Originality	Significance	Technical soundness	Clarity of presentation/language
Enter a score between 0 to 10	9	9	9	8	10

Final Evaluation

Excellent	Very Good	Good		Fair	Poor
Aceeptance	Minor Revision	Major Revision		Rejection	

THE BOOK ABOUT BRANKA

Branka was born in Trebinje on June 3, 1953, to father Radonja Đukić and mother Ilinka Đukić, née Zeković.

The Đukići, the ancestors on the father's side, were originally from the Pješivci tribe. They settled in Studence near Nikšić, after the Berlin Congress in 1878, when that area belonged to Montenegro. The Zekovići, the ancestors on the mother's side, came from the area around the villages of Tušina and Mljetičak, in Drobnjak. They moved and lived in Nikšić.

She moved to Titograd (Podgorica) in 1958 with her father, mother, and brother. Her father died in 1967 when she was 14 years old. She graduated from the "Savo Pejanović" Elementary School, the "Slobodan Škerović» Gymnasium, and the Faculty of Law in Titograd (Podgorica) in the regular term.

Immediately after graduating from law school, she got a job at "Zetatraans". She spent her working life in "Zetatrans" until her retirement on 12/30/2011.

BIRDHOUSE

Already on the seventh day, it rained
as if with me the whole world
was forgotten
but you smiled
and the sky smiled
at the same moment
And you flipped through your life
and the stars sparkled into my life
and then you kissed me
like a bird knocking on
your window

**I am celebrating the day of your love tonight in the
birdhouse, in the house for two**

And while I'm telling you about us,
you look at me and smile
because you know it all
Even though the days pass,
the birds still come
to our window

**I am celebrating the day of your love tonight in the
birdhouse, in the house for two**

Gabi Novak sings

Authors: Drago Britvić and Arsen Dedić,
Source: https://www.youtube.com/watch?v=0I2ckIXc7Zs
Licenses: [Merlin] Croatia Records (on behalf of Croatia Records), and 2 Music Rights Societies,
Podgorica,

I APPROACH THE WINDOW THROUGH THE CITY
WALKING AUTUMN

Forty years have passed in this condition on the sixth floor. It's autumn again. I moved, for the umpteenth time, the curtain at the right end of the window. In front of me, below, is the building of the Kindergarten "Đina Vrbica". The yard is fenced. Grass park with furniture. Slide, sand pool, metal bed with bars for children. They grasp the crossbar with their fists, higher above the ground, and move from one crossbar to another with the strength of their arm muscles. My three children finished attending this kindergarten a long time ago. I'm looking at him. It's hard for me to turn back and look around the apartment. I see her! I am aware of every detail of the apartment even when I am not in it. Living room. In the middle is a small, square, glass table, covered in disorder with several books and a notebook in which I write various notes, bills for used electricity, water, garbage collection, and apartment tax. In the corner of the room, a TV that I stopped turning on. I am fed up with what I have seen all these years, during which he did not move from that place, from that angle. Two couches against two opposite walls, two armchairs in which he can gently rock when he sits in them. On the wall, opposite the window, is a shelf with books and framed photos. Three drawers for documents, four cabinets, two at the top, and two at the bottom. In the lockers are binders with documents, diplomas, and certificates. Most of the documents have expired. They exist without meaning. There are also albums with pictures of events from life, which has passed, mostly, in these last forty years, my life and the lives of those who lived in this state. To the left is the dining room with a large round table, which has not been used for a long time for its basic purpose. On the right, by the wall, is the piano, on which the daughter practiced playing when she was a high school student.

To the left of the dining room, is a classic kitchen, separated from the dining room by a wall in the form of a bar. There is an electric stove, a refrigerator, a kitchen display case with a worktop, and more police on the walls, in which there are many dishes. I don't know how I would use it. My wife got it and sometimes used it when she prepared festive lunches for our grown children. The kitchen leads to a glazed balcony, which I also stopped going out to. Sometimes, very rarely, it happens to me that I take a step or two for a short time. In the second part of the apartment, there are two rooms, a small hallway, and a bath middle. The room, on the south side, towards Lake Skadar and the Adriatic Sea, has access to a small balcony, on which there are lines for drying clothes. I sleep in another room, on the north side, towards the hill of Gorica. It now has only one bed, two chests of drawers, and two bookshelves on the opposite walls of the room. The three-door wardrobe is in the right corner when you enter the room, leaning against two walls. It has a lot more wardrobe than I use. I don't know what to do with so many wardrobes. My movement in the state is mostly limited to lying on the couch in the living room, opening the fridge, eating at the bar counter, washing the dishes superficially, and going to bed for a night's sleep. It invigorates me when I happen to take an hour's nap, in the afternoon, in that bed. In the front of the apartment is a small hallway with a shelf for shoes on one wall, and across the street is a pantry with shelves on the wall, filled with objects, that I don't think I ever use. The utility room is dominated by a washing machine. I remember being here I bought it a long time ago and participated in its installation, but I have never used it personally. My wife used it. Now I will teach you to use it. So far, this storage room has been the most useful for storing my backpack with hiking equipment, hiking boots, and hiking poles. I'm tired of thinking that I should arrange, and clean the whole apartment and all the rugs in it. (10/19/2022)

◊

When you see everything, analyze, understand, and decide, you return to your apartment, where you are bound by memories and all emotions live in it. You have to live, look forward to each day that comes, and of course, remember the past. A man must not be alone but surrounded by people, children, grandchildren, and society, with the definition of life: "Everything that comes, I am next to it."

THE CHILD IS THE FATHER OF THE MAN

Figure 4. With Grandma (Gift of Stnka Zeković-Poleksić)

Figure 5. With cow (Gift of Stnka Zeković-Poleksić)

Did this little girl remain herself? Why does she need a watch on her wrist? Is she happy, without any reason, just by being there, next to the grandmother and next to the cow, on the outskirts of Nikšić? What does he offer to the grandmother, with an outstretched hand, in a small bowl? She is so big that she can freely stand next to the cow, hold the rope tied around the cow's horns with her left hand, and grab the cow by the neck with her right.

STUDENT AGE

Figure 6. On the Boulevard in front of the Post Office

Who is this beautiful, smiling, forgotten girl in high-heeled shoes, jeans, a plaid shirt, with glasses? Who are these guys? Why is everyone looking at her and everything revolves around her?

SUMMER OF 1977

Corso in Freedom Street. Summer vacation after the end of the last, tenth semester (graduate internship) at the Faculty of Electrical Engineering in Belgrade. I go out several nights in a row. I stand on the sidewalk across from the "Department Store" and observe. I'm looking. I am looking for a girl who will like me. I choose. Walkers pass from one end of the street to the other and back. I spotted a group of three girls. They walked together every evening.

One of them, on the side, was my friend from school, my generation, but I liked the girl in the middle. She was nicely sunbathed, with a tanned face. Blue blouse, white skirt, sandals. The most beautiful girl on the corso that summer. I started watching her, openly, every night. The girls noticed this and said to each other: "Željko is looking at you." I called my school friend and told her to introduce me to a friend she was walking with. She met us. We shook hands and went for ice cream on the terrace of Hotel "Crna Gora". I told her that I was studying. I told her that I had passed all the exams and that I was preparing my thesis. She told me that she has already graduated and is working.

She paid for the ice cream. She did not want to hear or allow another possibility.

Summer has passed and the month of January came very quickly. I looked for her and told her that I graduated. We went to the Green Lounge of Hotel "Crna Gora" to celebrate.

That's how it started

TIME OF MEASUREMENT

Figure 7 - On Duklja

Spring has arrived, so to speak, immediately. We scheduled meetings at the fountain in Ulica slobode. It is the only fountain in Freedom Street. In the upper part of the Street, across from the famous pastry shop Š.T. Hamza.

I usually wore light clothing, sports pants, a shirt, and a white sweater. Footwear, shoes that I really liked. Wide, comfortable yellow moccasins. Because of them, she called me "Yellow Duck".

We went on day trips to the sea by car. Around the city and its surroundings, on foot. One of those trips is the one in the picture, taken at the archaeological excavations in Duklja.

Did we measure up? Bearing in mind that, like this, she put her hand over my shoulder, and stood taller than me, it could be taken as a sure indication that we were measuring each other.

PREVIOUS TO THE WEDDING

Sometimes we used to take a taxi around the city. We were sitting in the back seat. On one occasion, our hands were on the seat, came close and touched. I felt it, and she also told me that she shivered from that touch.

I asked her, in the taxi: were you married, although I was sure of an affirmative answer.

She remained silent and confirmed that she would.

Preparations for the wedding have begun. She, with her friends, was choosing a wedding dress. She ordered a wedding dress from Ričard Gumzej from Zagreb. He was the most famous designer of wedding dresses in Yugoslavia. I was planning to be the groom in a white suit with a dark tie. And so it would.

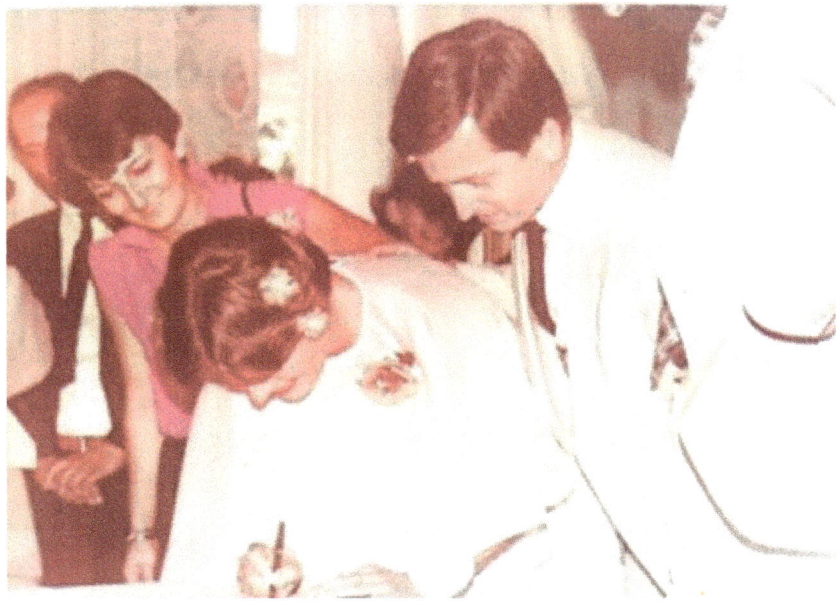

Figure 8 - The bride signs her name in the Marriage Book

HONEYMOON

We spent our honeymoon, in August 1980, on Hvar, for a week, at the "Solaris" auto camp near Šobenik, for a week, and on Bled, in Slovenia, for a week.

We left Tiotgarad by bus and arrived in Drvenik, a small town in southern Dalmatia, between Makarska and Ploče. The blue sky was dotted with reddish-ruddy clouds, which retained the reflections of the last rays of the setting sun. We managed to run into the last ferry, which, that day, was transporting passengers to Sućuraj on Hvar.

We slept in Sućuraj, and the next day, by bus, on a narrow, winding road, in the middle of the island, through the karst, waterless region with water cisterns in the fields, in some places, we headed to the town of Hvar. On the higher, steep elevations, there were thickets, very dense groups of low trees and tall bushes. On the lower slopes, thickets change to pine forests. We passed by Jelsa and Stari Grad and, after a few hours of driving, arrived in Hvar. Desired, targeted and challenging destination. Accommodation in a private house awaited us, previously secured through a tourist organization. The house was located high on the hill, with a view of the Hvar port, the town, and the surrounding area. A neat room with a double bed, fluffy, sparkling clean white sheets, and the smell of lavender in the room. In front of the house, the front part of the house, an open terrace with tables for serving meals. Fish and wine. Enjoyment. Food to enjoy. Fish, fis,h and wine.

Morning, early, departure to port. We buy two kilos of peaches, picked in the Neretva Valley, and brought them here for tourists to enjoy eating their juices.

The boatman took us to the island of Stipanska by boat. On the other side of the island, along a small bay, all naturally lined with stone, stepped slabs. All day sunbathing and swimming in clear, transparent sea water. Complete physical and mental rest. Paradise. Another world. In the evening, the boatman took us back to the port. From there to the host, dinner. Fish and wine. It was like that for three or four days. After that, the boatman suggested that we go swimming on the island of Jerolimo, a little closer to Hvar, right next to Stipanska island. We accepted. Beautiful beach, lots of bathers, view of the city and port, lots of sun and sea. Beauty and wonder. Seven days passed in a flash, but they remained unforgettable.

From the port of Hvar, we went by boat to Šibenik. Entering the beautiful bay of Sibenik was an event and experience of a special kind. My sister and brother-in-law were waiting for us. We spent the first night at their house. We were at the "Solaris" auto camp all day. During the day, sunbathe and swim on the beaches of "Solaris" and walk through the surrounding cypress park. Seven days. Seven days of sea, sun, lounging, and walking in the shade of cypress trees. Rest and recovery continue.

On the eighth day, in the evening, we got on the bus and headed along the Croatian coast to Slovenia, to Bled. In Bled, accommodation in a private house, with a woman whose husband had died not long before. Now she is engaged in tourism. Rural (peasant) tourism.

Lake Bled with Bled Castle is located on the only natural island in Slovenia. We rented a boat to ride on the lake, row to the castle and look around the castle. We walked around the lake.

They rode their bikes through the beautiful villages around the lake. Lots of greenery. Trees strewn with white flowers. I recorded everything with a camera so that the memory of those wonderful days would remain.

We set aside one day to visit Lake Bohinj, which is about thirty minutes away from Lake Bled. We went to the Savica waterfall, a double waterfall in the shape of the letter A. The water bursts out in the middle of the steep cliff wall and falls 78 meters into a wonderful, green pool. From there it continues along the stream of the same name, which, as the main source, flows into Lake Bohinj, and flows from Lake Bohinj as the source of the river Sava Bohinjka. After the Savica waterfall, that day we went up by cable car (gondola) in four minutes, from the shore of the lake to the ski station Vogel. From there, by cable car, to the last station, Orlova glava. From there, on foot, approximately one hour, to the mountain top of Sija. It was cold on that hill. We did not expect such cold and we were not prepared for it. Us in a light summer wardrobe. I gave Branka my sweater to ease her chattering teeth from November. We successfully returned back, by cable car.

The seventh, and last day of our stay in Bled is approaching. I carefully calculate how much money we have spent and make sure that we have enough left so that we don't have enough to return home.

We went to Zagreb from Bled, and from Zagreb, by plane, to Titograd. My mother and father were waiting for us at the airport.

The next day I rushed to the photographer to develop the film from the camera and take pictures, which I took all the time, from Drvenik, through Hvar, Solaris, Bled, Bohinj, Savica, Vogel... The photographer opened the camera lid and showed me. There was no film in the camera. I was surprised, stunned, and disappointed. The whole time I was taking pictures and clicking with an empty camera. Thus, from this honeymoon, not a single photo remained as a memory.

OWN FAMILY HOUSEHOLD

We rented an apartment in Vukice Mitrović Street, below Gorica, and started running a joint household. We bought food together, but she cooked and prepared the food. In the morning, we each went to our work, our place of work.

It was autumn. Two months have passed since the wedding. She started to welcome me and aggressively aimed at me.

Why am I not pregnant? My daughter-in-law immediately remained in a different state.

I was confused, taken aback, and surprised. Am I not the one who is in charge, who takes care of the pregnancy, and for whom the offspring is created? I did not expect something like this from my own wife.

The tension soon subsided because, the following month, she received a report from the doctor that she was pregnant.

For her, the doctor's report, and for me, pride and satisfaction.

◊

Summer came quickly. Grandpa Mijajlo came to Old Town. He stopped in front of the house, took out a gun from his gun, and fired three shots, high into the air, towards the sky. To burst, to resound, to be heard up to the sky! A male child was born! First, a man!

PRINCESS WITH FIRST BABY

Figure 9 – With his first-born son

NEW BEAUTIFUL BRENNA

We moved into the apartment in March 1983. It took three more months for the firstborn son to turn two years old, and a month and a half for the still-unborn daughter to be born. Branka's stomach had grown in the eighth month. She occasionally complained of lower back pain. I helped her lie down on the couch and massaged her back with my hands and an electric massager that we had bought. The pain did not stop. Somewhere, in the first days of May, I had the idea that it would be good to warm her back. This is how they work in physical therapy when they treat those with back pain. She lay down on the couch. I put a thick blanket on her back and passed over it with a heated iron to transfer heat to her. I don't remember if it was on the first or second day when she started screaming in pain. We rushed her to the hospital and she gave birth. The baby was born with thick, black hair, and the doctor on duty exclaimed: Here she is! New Beautiful Brena was born! So I, ironing with a hot iron, over the blanket, Branka's back, hastened that she would not stay too long in her mother's stomach, but that a daughter, New Beautiful Brenna.

VACATION TIME ON THE CROATIAN COAST

Summer of 1982, Hidden Port on Lastovo, and in 1984 Postira on Brač, Komiža on Vis, one day on Biševo, and Solaris near Šibenik.

Figure 10 – With daughter and son at Krka Falls

We were in Brač from August 3 to 17, 1985,
first in Milna (7 days) and then in Postira (7 days).
We swam in Osibova Bay. We visited Supetar, Bol,
and Splitska, and passed through Sumartin.
We climbed, Vido's mountain.

Bojana, Srđan, Branka i Željko
Postira, August 15, 1985.

RETURN TO THE MONTENEGRIN COAST FOR SUMMER VACATIONS

Summer 1987 on Jaz near Budva, and 1988 on Big beach near Ulcinj. I am satisfied. A happy father with his wife and children.

Figure 11 - With Zvjezdan on The Big Beach, Ulcinj

LAWYER IN WORK ORGANIZATION

In parallel with her family life, Branka very conscientiously worked as a lawyer in a labor organization. It impressed me. I loved having a wife like that.

In this picture, you can see the attentive expression on the face of a young, tidy employee with short hair, who calmly and purposefully follows and participates in the work conversation.

Figure 12—In the Legal Service and the Secretary of the Labor Organization

Employees in the work organization appreciated and respected her because of her work characteristics and human relationships with employees. I am looking at this photo from a fun-friendly evening, organized by Radna organization. I look at this smile, this face, these eyes, this long, white, folded scarf, draped over both shoulders, this dark dress... I loved such a woman.

Figure 13 – Fun Evening of the Work Organization

We leave the children at kindergarten, Branka goes to her workplace in her work organization, and I to mine, in my work organization. Completely different activities. After work, we return on time and pick up the children from kindergarten, and that's when family time and life in the apartment begins.

In my work organization, people were treated, and the scope of my work was medical devices. One segment within that framework was hemodialysis machines.

HEMODIALYSIS AND WORKER SELF-MANAGEMENT

Mid-eighties of the twentieth century. The Law on Collective Labor has been in society for ten years. Workers are sovereign to manage and dispose of the results of their work. The basic organization of joint work (OOUR) is the cell in which this is achieved. A complex organization of joint work (SOUR) unites several OOURs and related activities. The Workers' Council is the supreme body that decides on everything important for the work of OOUR. The external management body (director) acts alone, individually in various jobs, obligations, and competencies. He is elected by the Workers' Council. The gathering of working people is above all, the most massive, it is made up of all employees in the work organization. There is also Self-governing labor control to ensure that nothing wrong happens. One such Assembly of working people is held in the central hall, on the first floor, of the Main, New Hospital. A large number of employees. Among them is Elijah. The issue of what and where with the new hemodialysis department is being discussed and considered. Should it be in the Department of Urology or a separate Department of Nephrology? Elijah is thinking. What and how to decide. The introduction of hemodialysis in the The hospital was already designed and started by someone. Nobody asked him anything about it. Machines for hemodialysis, manufactured by "Gambro" and "Frezenius" under the self-governing "jurisdiction" of the work organization, belong to his service. That is why he cannot be indifferent while listening to the discussion, which has turned into a real polemic. The head of the Urology Department, a respected, eminent doctor, known far beyond the scope of the Hospital where he works and in which this issue is discussed at the assembly of working people, Vukotić ac. prim. dr Dagutin advocates the position that hemodialysis should be in the Urology Department because the highest level of development in kidney treatment has been achieved there, including chronic renal failure. On the other hand, a respected doctor, a specialist, Radović prim. Dr Rajko disagrees with this achievement and advocates the position that hemodialysis belongs to nephrology. Elijah, invisible to the point of non-existence, in the mass of busy people, cannot help but be surprised. What should he think or, God forbid, say, when two eminent doctors, specialists in the field of hemodialysis, do not agree but argue about this issue? The "victory" was won by a specialist with the opinion that hemodialysis should be done separately department of nephrology. In this way, in principle, new departments were created and new medical services were expanded in the hospital.

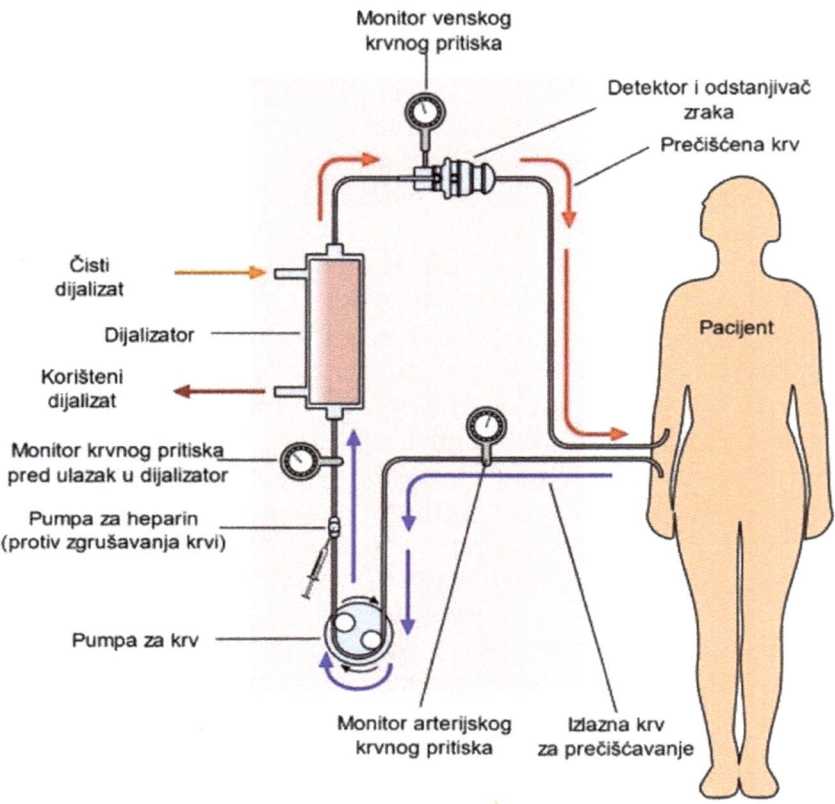

Figure 14 - Simplified Representation of Hemodialysis

"SCHOOL DOESN'T PAY FOR ANYONE"

At the beginning of that year in 1991, there was a general reorganization of the company, and thus of the work organization in which Elijah worked. The anemic Director, a sub-specialist for sick leave, was appointed as director. Work on the organization is an institution in the public sector and of public importance for Microcosm. Salaries for employees are determined according to the coefficient determined by the Ministry of Labor and Social Welfare of Microcosm. Logically, the highest coefficient for salary, that is, the highest salary, was received by the Anemic Director. He was appointed to that position by the Hepatobiliary Surgeon who applies knowledge from hepatobiliary surgery in the politics of the Microcosm, and the Hepatobiliary Surgeon was appointed to the position by the High Man Who Sees High Above the Microcosm.

Elijah, not bypassing the Anemic Director, demanded that the Ministry of Labor and Social Welfare determine the salary coefficient for him in the same way and according to the same principles that it determined for all employees. The Ministry did it, but, chirp! The Anemic Director got in the way and did not adopt the decision of the competent Ministry of Labor and Social Welfare. Wow!!!

Why? With his nose up high, walking around the table in the director's office, he asked Elijah: "Do you do this at our place? No one pays for school. "THEY" also have some specializations. Anemic Director from Martinići, the subspecialist for sick leave in his concentration camp, expressed his magnificent subspecialist contempt! "THEY" are the lower human species in the concentration camp of the Anemic Director, in which he planned to put Elijah as well. In the institution, it was said loud and clear: "The closer you are to the director, the higher your salary." Elijah also noticed one subspecialist, who, every morning, coming to work, first knocked on the door of the Anemic Director, to answer him, nodding his head and with a smile on his lips, and then went to the department where he was supposed to do his work.

The main task of the Hepatobiliary Surgeon, who, logically, did not do what he was trained for, operating on patients in the Operating Block, was to carry out Stalin's purges in Microcosm, and he did it more than successfully. The missing medical knowledge is paid for. He knew, among other things, from the position of Minister in Microcosm (government), to publicly warn a doctor, a pediatrician, and a deputy in the Assembly of Microcosm (opposition), to be careful what and how he says because he is both a Doctor and a Minister. "By the Code of Medical Ethics and Deontology, which was published approximately 19 years after that."[10] One could conclude that, at the time in question, there was no medical ethics. The pediatrician did not hesitate to admit: to being afraid! Minister - medical ethics has not been published yet. The question is, was there a force of law or a law of force?

Let's go back and remember: where was Elijah? Nowhere. What was he doing? Nothing. He was with a man who was prepared to, cold-bloodedly, "bring him thirsty across the water", to "row him over". The trap for excommunication had already been devised and set. "Scissors"!

Everyone is "transforming" and "reforming", the whole society, the entire work organization, only Elijah has no place in the reforms. Let him fall unreformed! He is a lower human species? A heretic? No Pasaran!

The assistant to the Minister of Labor and Social Welfare, who made the decision, clearly said: "There is no goodwill". So, there is a bad will, the bad will of the evil Anemic Director and the unknown labor organization.

Elijah has too long retention. He was telling a story to the deaf.

"At the medical faculty, human health is viewed from a biological point of view. They separate the mind from the body, they don't see the connections, they don't see the interaction. They don't see or teach you how mind-body interactions affect psychological health, despite all the research surrounding us for many decades.

They also separate the individual from the environment. They do not introduce social factors, such as race, inequality, economic status, and oppression, the stress in a society that affects all individuals. On the contrary, they claim that everything is just a matter of biology. None of that is biology! When it comes to trauma, which is a huge factor in all mental health problems, as well as most chronic physical illnesses, the average medical student doesn't even hear a lecture on trauma, but none. So, during practice, I had to look at all these connections, and when I looked at them, I realized that there were a lot of doctors and researchers who saw them, but no one told me anything about it." [7]

"Is that man still alive", asks Elijah's daughter. "Why do you mention him?" Do you hate him and thus poison yourself? Are you

---

10   Code of medical ethics and deontology, Medical Chamber of Montenegro, Podgorica, 2009.

jealous? Do you envy him for what? Did he owe you anything?" "No", answers Elijah. "It's a memory. The scar of life." Chronic posttraumatic syndrome came before it. Elijah has his own "Safe place" where he can move away from the trauma and continue to live on. The soul is truly healed by forgetting.

Pigwash. Together with the Minister of Health, who appointed him, and the Director of the Health Fund, whom the Minister also appointed, he brought from the already defunct Radoje Dakić Factory. Interesting! Regardless of this triumvirate of functionaries, the Earth continues to rotate on its axis and around the Sun, and the tilt of its axis has not changed, almost not a bit. "Let flowers spring up on their cemetery for a distant generation, like everyone who has the law in their hands, their traces stink of inhumanity."[11]

For a man to satisfy all his needs, he has to contact various people, both wanted and unwanted. „Who is the neighbor Elijah, the Anemic Director, the Hepatobiliary Surgeon?" Do you think that Microcosm exists only in this book?"

---

12 Petar II Petrović Njegoš, „Mountain Wreath", Obod, Cetinje, 1996.

"You gave gifts, but you stole
And you were unfaithful to me
You didn't give me too much
O youth, O youth,
O my youth.

That stingy sun that shone,
That poor love, short dreams,
For memories that's a little,
About youth, youth

So goodbye, be better with another,
And give him more tenderness,
Because it's nothing that I lose,
About youth, youth. "

Author: Arsen Dedić, Oh, youth
https://www.podijeli.net/tekstovi/arsen-dedić/o-mladosti/2709

ONE LETTER DATED OCTOBER 12, 1991. YEARS

Taking upon ourselves the obligation to write a professional, objective, and as useful letter as possible for you, we found ourselves faced with a certain dilemma of whether to comment only on the facts presented in your letter, or to try to find out some items that you did not mention, but somehow imply. We decided to stay on the platform of facts, which we hope you will use objectively, usefully, and above all adequately to get out of your current problems.

There is no doubt that the problems of the family in general will become more and more prominent because this is imposed by the social, political, and economic climate. Of course, it is impossible to speak in general, in the form of a solid and strictly defined scheme. But it is obvious that you also formed a more or less transformed, but still patriarchal family with established family relationships. However, we should not lose sight of the fact that family relationships change - as the years of marriage go by, as children grow up and impose their own rules of the game. Problems, discomforts, and difficulties arise because people and their understandings change much more slowly than the new family structure. An important item is also a stable economic situation, which, in your case, seems to be satisfied. We emphasize this because, you will agree with us, that changes in the material and economic basis of the family are often a condition for changing the entire family structure and its relationships.

In the personal life of an individual, it is normal that the importance of the family is great. However, the increase in the family causes qualitatively different relations among its members. The positive thing is that each individual in the extended family is increasingly enriched as a person. But, with the increase in the number of members, the obligations of all members also increase. Very often, spouses who, at the beginning of their marriage, were completely devoted to each other, drift apart. On the other hand, strong bonds are created between the woman (mother) and the children.

You are satisfied that your wife is a good mother, but you found yourself in a situation for which you were not sufficiently prepared - that your wife is moving away from you. The stage of neglecting your spouse (in this case – you) hides the danger that the spouse will become too distant, that there will be emotional coldness, intolerance, infidelity, and, in the worst case, the disintegration of the family. Since the relationship between you and her changes significantly, your connection weakens, and the common thread is lost. Our time brought the emancipation of women and gave women new rights, but also increased obligations. You are starting from a bad position if you are looking for the culprit in you or her. No one is to blame for such events. Such changes occur when something major happens, when one of the parties simply "bursts" from dissatisfaction, or if, on the contrary, nothing happens for a long time, and the monotony of everyday life simply causes such reactions in both you and your wife.

Looking from her point of view, things probably look like this - she is burdened with daily responsibilities at work, at home, and towards her children, and is dissatisfied with the environment (first of all - you, because you are the most important to her) does not notice how much she has done and her efforts and that makes room for feelings of loneliness. Grumbling, and nervousness, sighing... that's her alarm, a cry for help. Or, even better, it wants to tell you through humming:

"I need protection, comfort, love, attention!" Notice me, understand me, love me - that's what's most important to me!" You seem to lack the power of perception. As the day goes on, you do not respond to her requests and normally the result is that she is punished with sexual abstinence. You don't understand it and - the circle closes. You two are in a deaf war. So where is the exit? The message, it seems to us, is clear - don't walk away! Try to organize an evening just for the two of you every once in a while. Take a walk along the old paths, sit in the restaurant where you started to cultivate your love, sit at home reminiscing about old experiences that meant a lot to you... And try to be as gentle as possible. Hand in hand - and all problems will, over time, disappear. This kind of behavior will bring happiness to you and your wife, and of course to your children too - there will be no shouting and arguments and family relations will become more harmonious.

Responsibility for your behavior is mutual, but - start first. When someone is almost 40 years old, with a higher education, then he is certainly aware that maturity and responsibility should be the basic model of behavior. Give your wife small, small pleasures during the day. Believe me, women need a little. Use small "men's tricks". Remember how it worked for you when you were busy and promised eternal and only love? Leave all obligations for a moment and calmly, together, drink coffee, and talk. Sometimes compliment her on her new hairstyle, and shoes, or give her some other compliment. She is crying out for attention. She is probably tired of washing, ironing, and cooking, that in the background, without praise. Is love an art? If so, it requires knowledge and effort, not something that is born by chance.

Your wife and you are entering a state that can be described as "hunger for love". Remember - women always try to be attractive, dress up, and take care of themselves... So start winning over your woman and start pleasant conversations, showing goodwill and understanding her.

Often you are not aware of how problems accumulate, so you find yourself in a situation where the circle is closed. Then the struggle begins - how to get out of the vicious circle. The consequence of such a condition is headaches, which are certainly Psychosomatic. As the knot unravels and you and your wife reestablish intimate emotional contact, sedatives, and major headaches should be a thing of the past. Man's desire for a relationship in an emotional and certainly sexual sense is the strongest. The impossibility of its satisfaction often leads to illness (ulcers, headaches...). Live together, you need each other, so enrich your own life and stop punishing each other. Enjoy yourself, your family, and all that you have achieved. If you don't take action, you will make yourself feel helpless. Giving must be mutual. The only condition for achieving that harmony between two people is complete emotional closeness. At the same time, for you, as a man, the proof of that closeness is sexual intercourse, and for your wife, as a woman, the proof is a nice word, physical closeness, praise for her appearance, and the effort she puts in. , and for her sexual intercourse comes later - as a result of the satisfaction of all those factors, but also the peak of pleasure.

Giving is never and can never be deprivation, sacrifice, or abandonment of another. Giving is an experience of one's strength and enrichment. It would be painful and futile to live together and not give. Everyday experience tells us that what a man considers a need depends a lot on his character. You are there to determine, knowing your wife, what she needs, and when. When you're both in the mood for an open conversation, without outsmarting, or worse, physical competition, talk openly about your intimate life, your hopes and fears. Even showing anger, hatred or impatience is much better than separation, silence... Mixed, ambivalent feelings are common among marriage partners and are tolerated as long as there is a tendency to grow into positive feelings. You will agree that one cannot be intimate only in bed. Sexual desires must be connected with the emotion of love. Your wife wants the desire for physical be combined with your attention and love for her. Otherwise, after the relationship, she will feel like a "thing", used and misunderstood, and each time she will move further away from you. Tenderness is an integral part of love - both in physical and non-physical forms of love. Loving someone is not only a strong feeling - it is also a decision and a promise.

Taking everything into account, we can conclude that you have many chances that you can use to achieve the success is complete and final.

The team at the psychological counseling center sends you and your family lots of success, happiness, and mutual understanding.

◊

The psychologist's advice was useful. Happiness returns to the family nest. Children are growing up, and Elijah is getting old.

GUESTS AT A WEDDING IN BELGRADE

Figure 15 - Arrival at the Wedding, Belgrade, 2005

Broad smiles, joy in the chest, and pride overwhelmed the mother and son as they solemnly walked, approaching a new celebration, at which the new bride will ceremoniously receive a wedding ring on an open stage in Košutnjak, in front of guests, dignitaries, arrived from Bosnia and Herzegovina, Montenegro and Serbia. Beauty and joy pervade mother and son at this wedding in Belgrade.

Figure 16 - Dance at the wedding

Branka and I, husband and wife with already a long marriage record, are calm. Side by side and side by side. Our dance is light. Hand in hand. My arm around her waist, hers over my shoulder. All around us is a noisy rejoicing. Our peace and contentment are deep within us.

Figure 17 - Montenegrin jump. The bridge got married.

Completely uninvited, provoked by nothing from the outside, an unstoppable enthusiasm to dance, to jump Montenegrin at another wedding in Belgrade, on a boat on the Sava, near the confluence of the Danube, boiled out of me.

I look at this picture and rejoice. My heart and soul rejoice as I fly. I fly, fly, fly...

THE CHILDREN HAVE GROWN UP

"My dear, I don't know how long I've been standing here, I'd love to go back." You don't know that half of me stayed with you to follow you. My love, you are tired and without you I am preparing a bed for you on some star that is going out, I am looking for the light that I do not have."

Figure 18–Excursion to Virpazar

A beautiful day. Clear and sunny. Hand in hand, side by side. Smiles on your face. Look straight at the one who is looking at us.

THE FIRSTBORN SON IS GETTING MARRIED

Figure 19 – Ode to Joy

That day has come. The first baby, the eldest son grew up and got married. The happy mother looked up, and embraced both sons in a wide hug, with wide smiles, wide, wide joy and happiness in her chest.

It was the best wedding in the "Podgorica" Hotel.

"It will be easy for you to do without me,
but how will I do without you
when the hard days come
when all the friends leave
when they smell lilacs."

Figure 20 - Ode to Joy

Mother and daughter. Daughter and mother. The widest and tightest hug at the first wedding in the family.

UNTIL WE MEET AGAIN

The star has arrived. The time has come for him to get married too. A happy mother dances with her son at a wedding. Smiling, happy and joyful, she looks into his eyes. She gave birth to him and raised him to be able to create and support his family.

Figure 21 – Dans with Zvjezdan for eternity

These "Odes of Joy" could not last long. That beauty of our lives acts as an illusion, as a calm before the storm.

MORSE IN TABULA

(Exitus lethal at 14:45h)
UNIVERSITY CLINICAL CENTER OF SERBIA
CLINIC FOR CARDIOVASCULAR SURGERY
INTENSIVE CARE DEPARTMENT
Treated since August 13, 2022. until 18.08.2022.

DISCHARGE LIST WITH EPICRISIS

Diagnosis: Stenosis valvulae mitralis non rheumatic

Signed by: Director of the clinic, Prof. Dr. Svetozar Putnik, cardiac surgeon; Head of the department, Ass. Dr. Ilija Bilbia, cardiac surgeon;

Presiding physician, Ass. Dr. sci med Duško Terzić, a cardiac surgeon.
Seal: Republic of Serbia - Belgrade

Massive endocarditis of the mitral and aortic valves was diagnosed intraoperatively. The infectious process affected the entire subvalvular apparatus of MV. After the first attempt to separate the patient from the ECC, there is a drop in tension. The patient was returned to the mode of maximum work of ECC with the inclusion of maximum inotropic support. After prolonging the ECC, with maximum inotropic support, the patient was gradually weaned from the ECC. The competence of the replaced valves was verified by the TEE examination.

Checked hemostasis. After the closure of the sternum, hemodynamic instability occurred again, the sternum was urgently opened, and heart massage was started. All applied resuscitation measures remain without an adequate response.

Mors in tabula (Exitus lethalis at 14:45) is declared.

A clinical autopsy is not required.

◊

The casket with the remains arrived at the chapel on Čepurci around nine o›clock in the evening. I hugged the dead coffin for a long time, sobbing bitterly and painfully.

The Zvjezdan was next to the wall, turning around, spinning, fiddling, sobbing loudly and bitterly.

BELOVED BRANKA,

I didn't know, I didn't believe, I didn't think that this was the end, that a disease had come that has no cure and that will take you away, however, too quickly. I believed and hoped that it would be different, even when I was listening to you, sitting across from you, as you uttered the words, "Alone! Alone!" I will do it myself!"

Where? Where are you going alone? On the road of no return. To death.

The thought that you will never again, after 42 years, enter our apartment, our house, your house, gives me stomach cramps and pain in my whole body.

Instead of arrivals and meetings, instead of everything, we got you, we have you packed in a coffin so that we never see, hear, or feel you alive again. Neither you nor us. You neither hear nor see.

There is only a picture of you with a wide smile, big teeth, and scattered hair for all those who knew you and for whom you were once a living being and a respected person, because of your deeds.

I wish you a better world and a better society than I was for you. It's fun for me!

I cry for you, my Branka. Leleeeeeeeeek !!!!!

Today and foreveeeeeeeeeeeer !!!!!

Željko Vujović Podgorica,
20.08.2022.

"Why are you gone? Why are you gone?"
When on young field flowers
Silent midnight strings a pearl
The song flows through my chest
Why aren't you there, why aren't you there".

Figure 22 - Wide smile, big teeth, scattered hair

Figure 23 – "To die is to have no need for another being."

I have been reading the document "Discharge list with epicrisis" for a long time. Analyzed it, studied it. I wanted to annul it as the lowest legal act. I wanted to find out that the cardiac surgeons from the University of Cardiac Surgery Clinic in Belgrade were sloppy. They changed the heart valves mechanically, like spark plugs on a car. That they didn't do everything they were supposed to do., instead of life, they sent me a death certificate.

I can't figure out how that happened. I would like to deny that massive endocarditis of the mitral and aortic valves was diagnosed intraoperatively and that the infectious process affected the entire subvalvular apparatus MV.

I cannot understand that the heart has completely disintegrated, that it cannot do what it exists for, that is, what it existed for.

I am silent. I stare blankly at the pictures on the wall in the living room, in the apartment, which Branka chose and installed to decorate the apartment.

"THE SOUL IS HEALED BY FORGETTING"

In my mind is the confirmation from the University of Cardiac Surgery Clinic in Belgrade that she died. There. At their place. I don't know where that certificate is now. I put it away somewhere. It fools me. Again, the crazy idea that confirmation is the lowest legal act, that death requires a much higher legal act, is running through my mind. Every time I enter the apartment, she seems to be there. In the living room, on the couch, he goes through the dining room, the hallway, and the room, to the balcony to spread the laundry. You can't see her, you can't hear her, but, so invisible and silent, she walks around the apartment.

In the cottage, on Durmitor, as well. The last time I was there, I didn't see her on the couch in the living room and I had a big crying fit. From there, where she went, no one came back. I am not yet aware that she has left. I hold her, somewhere inside me, as if she is better there. I create an appearance, an illusion. I live in an illusion. How can I forget her? It is easy for her now that she is in the Street of those who are not disturbed by anyone. I'm going out on the town. It's a clear autumn day. Everything is the same. Houses and unknown people pass through the streets of my city. Something tightens in my throat. I feel a pain in my chest.

THE WOMAN AND THE PSYCHIATRIST

People say that a professor's husband, who was a psychiatrist, died. After that, she went to his grave for a long time, threw stones at the grave, threw stones at the grave, and cursed loudly: Your mother's cunt! Why did you leave me?! Why?!!!

SADNESS

Grief is a reaction to the loss of something precious, and important, to which the individual attaches special importance. A normal response to the loss of a loved object.

A HERO OF OUR AGE[12]

"There are moments in life when your neighbor separates from you like a nail from the thumb on the right hand and leaves." You are then all reduced to one single gesture, one motive, and one emotion, which is falsely displayed through thousands of intermediate feelings: you are reduced to that futile and profoundly unreasonable attempt to return him. What happens in such moments, on that day, maybe on the weekend, or in more invasive cases, in those months and years, is one of your strongest experiences in life. You are present in it as much as you could not be at the time of your birth and as much as you will not be at the time of your death.

For the community, death is something ordinary and every day. It's the same for you until your loved ones die. Moreover, the more unusual the death, the more sudden it is, the more the death is caused by an internal accident and not by external actions, and the more the community will instinctively distance itself from you. Formal expressions of condolence serve this distance: when someone says you accept my condolence, they usually mean get away from me. That's what hospital forms are for, rules of behavior in the morgue, post-mortem police reports... The system didn't let you down in your desperate attempts to get your loved one back, to get the nail on your right thumb back, but some living people avoided it. your destiny rewrites them. In a way, it's a good thing that it is, because you will

---

12   Lermontov Mihail Jurjevič, Hero of our Age, "Veselin Masleša", Sarajevo, 1974.

console yourself by telling yourself that they are to blame for the death of your loved one. What would you do without that comfort? How would you explain this loss to yourself?"

SEMIOTICS OF DARKNESS AND SEMANTICS OF SILENCE[13]

A man named Uve[14] was returning yesterday from Delta City, passed the Big River over the Crooked Bridge, and continued along the street towards Zabjelo, passed the football stadium, turned left onto the road leading to Ljubović, came to a metal gate with bars, and entered Street of those who are not disturbed by anyone.

Clear, sunny, November day. Marble headstones with gilded names. Again, he failed to simply find grave site number 262, plot 11, which he bought with his father's power of attorney and his father's money, in the summer of the penultimate year of the last, twentieth century. He was following path number 10. He did not see the fountain, which was his landmark to find the burial place he was looking for. Search. The fountain is in track number 11. It goes from track number 10 to track number 11, stepping on the green grass between the marble tombstones. See the fountain. He heads towards her. Turning left, stepping on the green grass again, he comes to the marble tombstone at grave site number 262. Dark marble. Two pots with flowers. Around the grass. The letters of Branka's name still shine. Fathers and mothers have darkened. He puts his hand on the marble slab, looks up to the sky, and sighs deeply. It will stay a little longer. Fix the position of one pot with flowers. He straightened up, sighed once more, several more times, and slowly headed towards the chapels and the exit towards Montenegrin Serdar Street. His gaze wanders in all directions. He will not stop at the names of people, who were once living beings, written on the monuments. There is a large number of those he knew. He suppresses from his mind, from his memory, the names of those three evildoers from the time he worked at the Medical Institute. Their marble tombstones are in the same plot number 11, across the street from the fountain. Among the other tombstones, he can distinguish them located at the vertices of a large acute-angled triangle. Perhaps, a little, they stand out compared to the others, because their marble is darker. They are the source of darkness. "The impression is the experience of a lack of light. The day is clear, the sun

---

13   Slavica Perović, "Life Lift", New book, Podgorica 2012, p.
14   Fredrik Bakman, "A man named Uve", New book, Podgorica, 2018

is shining. The inclination of the earth in its path around the sun is almost unchanged. Where did that hint of darkness come from?"

Exited through the gate closer to Ljubović, to the chapel, continued along the sidewalk of Montenegrin Serdar Street to the intersection with traffic lights near the "Sergije Stanić" Vocational School. Across the street from the school is now a hotel "Union", built on the spot where the family house of his long-deceased neighbor Ilija Stanić used to be. He does not stop by the house that he inherited from his father and mother. The house is there, quite close, in the middle of a small, quiet, quiet street, hidden by newly built multi-story buildings. He crosses the intersection and continues straight, to the end of the Boulevard, to his apartment on the sixth floor. He has not yet accepted or understood that he will be alone in the apartment and that he is single. His children stopped being children a long time ago. They don't have, they don't feel the need to contact him, call him, do something, or clean up something in the apartment, which, for many years, was also their apartment, their home. They have their apartments. They separated. He's thinking. He is always the one who calls them first. He keeps them there, somewhere in himself, in his throat, in his chest. He doesn't drop them. He cannot let them go, even though they have long since left, separated.

Silence. A man named Uve is lying in bed. Wake up. He opens his eyes. It hasn't been distributed yet. He feels bad. His nose is blocked. Common cold. He will cancel his participation in today's hiking tour in the Kučki mountains, below Treskavac to Bukumir Lake. He looks over the walls of the room, and the furniture. Everything is there, the same as it was when Branka left. The beds in the former matrimonial room were unmoved. On them, several plastic folders, left there temporarily, in an attempt to organize the chest of drawers by the window. Plastic bags filled with clothing intended for the Red Cross, leaning against the wall, are waiting. The wardrobe is not sorted yet.

What should he do?

Gets up. He makes tea. No one answers him. No one calls him. Will he call the children? To ask if he will come to visit them today.

He gave up.

YOU NEED TO LOOK IN THE MIRROR ONCE[15]

Look deeply into the mirror,
into the reflection of yourself.
That you look with your eyes open is not a lie,
it is not a poetic metaphor. That's you.
With the name your mother gave you, do you remember?
You, with the identity of success and defeat. Loss.
Unfulfilled and unfulfilled dreams In search of peace with thoughts
that swarm like bees in hives in an apiary.
Do you see that face? Dark circles, gray hair?
A calm, wrinkled forehead between the eyes?
Vague and vague chest tightness?
Tonight will be the New Year.
The first one, which she won't wait for.
People pass by on the street, through markets, cafes...
Emptiness in the chest. Emptiness and quiet sadness.
The great loneliness returns to consciousness.
A terrible feeling of helplessness.
She didn't bother anyone, and she had to go.
Forever.
It needs to be studied again.
To learn to enjoy oneself.
In himself and silence.
The relationship with the family should be nurtured.
The extended family is a resource.
Family history and contact with distant relatives remind one that one's
own life is part of a larger story with many interesting characters.
Bert Hellinger is your father's age.
He was born the same year as your father
He lived 21 years longer than him.
What is your family schedule like?

---

15   Pietra Von Thielen, Poetry and Prose, "Female Mirror", Split, Dalmatia, Croatia, on
31.12.2022.

Figure 24 – This is how the last year of the seventh decade of the twentieth century was welcomed in the House of the JNA in Podgorica

A year and a half has passed since that summer of 1977. Look at this conceited but confident guy with his nose and chin up and thisbeautiful girl with a big smile and blonde hair looking up at him.

She doesn't seem to begrudge him his conceit. Maybe he's not conceited, he's just happy and satisfied that this beautiful girl is next to him.

This girl has it all. She radiates beauty and joy to the environment, and to those who are around her.

Where did this bright figure go?

Figure 25 - Branka at the dawn of New Year 1979

01.01.2023.

◊

I dreamed of her before dawn.
The kind with bangs
like on a trip to Virpazar.
She was getting ready to go somewhere.
I asked her: Where are you going?
She didn't want to say.
I was spinning around her.
So tell me, at least, for God's sake!
She didn't tell me. I woke up.

06.01.2023

Is this enough evidence for a person to come to terms with the fact that someone is no longer there? Many things are argued with someone over time, and what is a man?

And what will I do and how will I do it?
Little hands, little strength,
straw among the whirlwinds[16].

◊

"Well, my friend:

There comes a moment in life when you establish:

who is important to you, who was never important to you, who will never be important to you again, who will always be important to you!

So don't worry about people from your past, because there's a reason why they didn't included in your present.

Happiness makes you better. Temptation makes you stronger. Grief makes you a man. Failure makes you humble.

Only the strength of your personality pushes you towards success and progress."

Glory and memory to my Branka!

Podgorica, February 18, 2023

---

16   Petar II Petrović Njegoš, Mountain wreath, Obod, Cetinje, 1996.

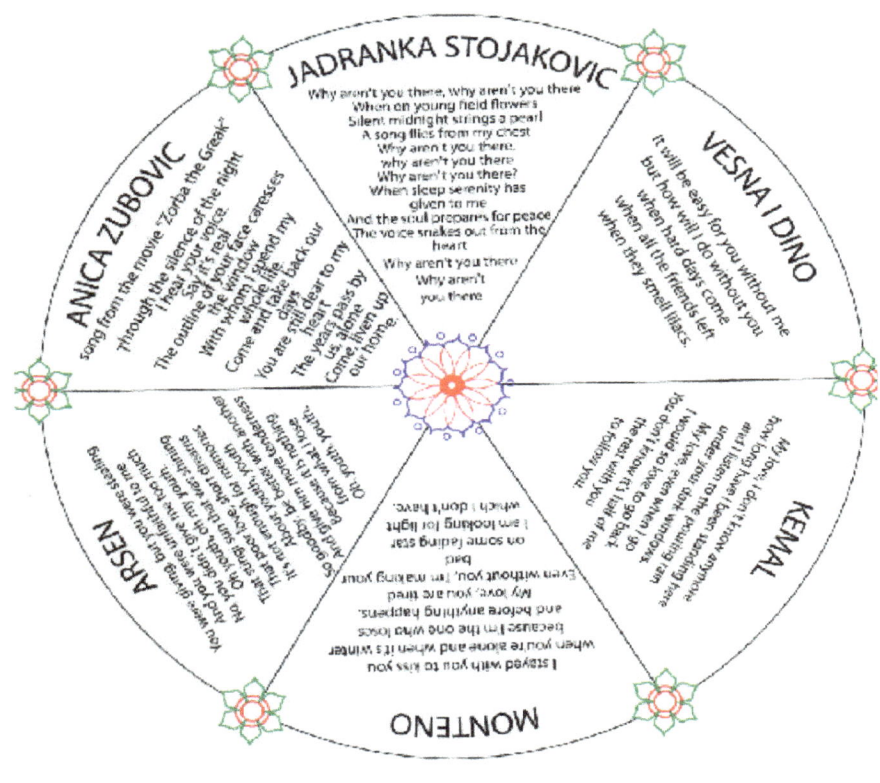

CAROUSEL

There is no solution in destruction. Life is a carousel, it should be a game. What does the song "Bird House", sung by Gabi Novak, and what does the song "Igra bez granica", performed by Toše Proeski, relate to?

Željko Vujović

December 12, 2023

GAME WITHOUT LIMITS

If only they could wake up in the world of love without my old friends and these freaks who always followed me.

If only I could kiss you without bad memories of the cold spring without the image of suffering that sticks with us

Because my life is a game without limits, a tired story, tearing pages on which nothing is written

Because my life is an eternal fall, when I add up the defeats, nothing remains, I'm still dragging my habits and that's all there is to it.

If only I could wake you up, make your coffee, bring you to bed, and kiss you, but that doesn't exist.

If only I could fall in love with a little village girl in some clearing up in space so I can't see down there

Because my life is a game without limits,

a tired story,

a tearing of pages on which nothing is written

Because my life is an eternal fall,

when I add up the defeats, nothing remains,

I'm still dragging my habits and that's all there is to it.

Sung by Toša Proeski

Author of music: Miroslav Rus Author of lyrics: Miroslav Rus
Author of arrangement: Nikša Bratoš Video clip for the song "Game with no limits" from the promotion of the album "Game with no limits The factory, Zagreb.
Source: https://www.youtube.com/watch?v=VMT50KhLlRw
License: [Merlin] IDJDigital (on behalf of City Records), and 4 Music Rights Societies License: CC BY 4.

THE IMMORTAL SOUL

„If the East gives birth to the bright Sun,
If the being boils in bright rays,
If Earth is not an apparition,
The human soul is immortal."

THE SPACE IS SMALL,
AND THE TIME IS GREAT

Alexa

"IN THE CHAOTIC MURMUR OF AN UNCLEAR DESTINY"

by Željko Vujović

In the autobiographical novel, Željko Vujović seems to be moving in a quiet sailing ship not far along the mainland and observes everything on the shore. With the calmness of an objective analyzer, he notices all the details, in the style of top masters. He sees the houses on the coast, the sailors, looks into the apartments, examines the furniture... He looks very precisely at a long past time and presents it to the reader as if it happened right now. How often does that cold-blooded calm give way to a somewhat emotional subjective assessment? Then the figure of the Anemic Director appeared who was "appointed to that position by the Hepatobiliary Surgeon who applies the knowledge of hepatobiliary surgery in the politics of the Microcosm, and the Hepatobiliary Surgeon was appointed to the position by the Tall Man Who Sees High through the Microcosm." That emotional assessment is contained in a mild edge of irony which only reinforces the image of society that we survived a long time ago.

And, again, after a touch of irony, a meaningful narration. The minister, lacking medical knowledge, was appointed to threaten those who know their job, for which they should be paid. That is why he, the Minister, works so heartily and enthusiastically on Stalin's purges. The pure reality that we almost forgot!

Then a death in the family. Death of a beloved wife. Something irreplaceable. Something he has to deal with for the rest of his life. "He has not yet accepted or realized that he will be alone in the apartment, that he is single." His children are they stopped being children a long time ago. They don't have, they don't feel the need to contact him, call him, do something, or clean up something in the apartment, which, for many years, was also their apartment, their home. They have their apartments. They separated. He's thinking. He is always the one who answers them first. He keeps them there, somewhere in himself, in his throat, in his chest. He doesn't drop them. He can't let them go, even though they have long since left, separated."

That's the painful truth. The heart of the couple. (Even if someone's health is broken, medically without hope of recovery, he alone, his children, dear ones, and one across the "big pond"! It seems a universal living truth.) All he has to do is hold them and don't let go "in the throat, in the chest."

Željko is the treasure of many generations before him, so his novel Is a family chronicle, written truthfully, collected, and factual. Sometimes he breaks into a biting caricature: The Running Pissing Man. But it is a testimony of the times we lived in, maybe we forgot, but it comes back to us again and again: bad students educate respectable professors. And those respectable "beat the stone" on Goli Otok. "Why? For nothing." Answers the stout old woman, carrying on her mare a full "carload" of grapes and figs, which she picked with her own hands and laboriously and intended for her son and grandchildren, pointing with her head to the house of Blaž Jovanović, who, at that time, was cheering and dressing in Montenegro. The work covers wide areas of psychoanalysis,sociology, poetry, pain, and overcoming historiography...

And so, sailing noiselessly on the sailboat, Željko scans everything around him. He looks far across the shore and dives into the deposits of the family saga, paving the way to the truth. With that, he immortalized his family.

In the end, to paraphrase Miloš Crnjanski, in Migrations, the second book says: "There are migrations. There is no death!" I will say: "There is life, there is no death!".

JELENA PETROVIĆ[17]

Dear Željko,

My opinion is that with this book you want to pay tribute to your beloved wife.

In Montenegro, where for a long time the main literature was about depressed Montenegrins, a book that pays tribute to a deceased wife is a real revolution. That's why I support her writing.

I also support writing the book as a woman, because I know how challenging it is to be a wife, a mother, an employee, to pick up all the threads, tie them into a ball called Family, and to be and remain happy in all of this. Dear Željko, believe me, a woman influences a family a lot. A lot depends on her in the home. A wise woman, as your wife certainly was, knew this very well, and this knowledge is not an easy task for a woman. A wife and mother know that happiness in the home literally depends on her, and then she has to create and build that happiness... because she loves her family. It used to be understood that the husband creates a roof over the head, but what is under the roof is mostly created by the woman. The roof is what is seen and what everyone admires and respects, but what is under the roof - peace, well-being, harmony, health, togetherness ... is what largely depends on the woman, and that is a great task that requires a great effort.

I'll tell you a secret. My grandmother left me, as a little girl, a watch as an inheritance, saying that one day, when I grow up, I won't be late for a date with a guy. I see, when your wife was a little girl, her grandmother left a watch as an inheritance.

March 1, 2023.

---

17   Jelena Petrović is the editor and founder of the Internet and Facebook page "Blue Star".

ESSAY ON SOFIA

Željko, I looked through the manuscript, but, apart from the title, nothing is right here. Books of this type[18] should not include medical reports that talk about someone's private life.[19] The book needs to be refined and completely reshaped. Let it be your memory of the moments spent with your wife. You should provide a lyrical portrait of her. This way, you have mixed up frogs and grandmothers. From the essay on loneliness, at the beginning, which would have been good if you had continued, to the genealogy of the family, photos, letters, and medical reports that are tasteless[20], and inappropriate.[21]

Delete the note on the first page that no one has copyright over your book because that is understood, and how would they have when it comes to your intimate confession?[22] Instead, put the thought of a great writer, at least the one whose quote you titled the work after or another.

I understand your idea, but the artistic realization is not good. You added, for God's sake, that the woman had an abortion. People would resent you, that's not for publication![23]

When and where did you meet, the past of her family, love, marriage, the birth of your three children... You have a lot to write about. Eventually her death. There should be more text, more living flesh, impressions, memories, and emotions. You go from an essay to a historical story, from it to photographs, from them to reports, and finally letters from readers. These are contributions of different genres, which do not go together.[24] You should read more autobiographies and biographies.[25]

If you start with a loneliness essay, which is not bad, then you should go in retrospect, to tell the readers the story of your love.[26] You are very good at writing essays. From the first essay on loneliness,

---

18   What kind of book is this?
19   Why can't they? Who and where prescribed that ban?
20   How and what flavor should be added to medical reports to make them palatable? What flavor do delicious medical reports have?
21   How are medical reports changed to be appropriate?
22   What is the purpose of suppressing and reducing the book to an intimate confession?
23   Why should people blame me for that? Why is it not for publication? Who restricts my posting and why?
24   Why don't they go together?
25   Why? What will it do for me to read more autobiographies and biographies?
26   Why? What will the story about my (our) love mean to the readers?

go back in time. You send me 5 - 6 essays about your acquaintance, love, and society, but let there be a lot of atmosphere. Remove the first page about authorship, historical genealogies, letters from readers, and medical reports. This is included only in critical books, not in biographies.[27] After all, you can also write about that abortion, but then describe your feelings[28] at that moment, but not through a medical report.[29]

◊

Sofia is right and she made an excellent assessment that nothing is wrong here, except for the title. The book needs to be refined and completely reshaped. Turn into a critical book.

A critical book is a work of literature, philosophy, or other academic disciplines that offers a detailed and thorough analysis and assessment of a particular subject or topic. This type of book usually involves an in-depth examination and critique of ideas, arguments, and theories, and seeks to provide a comprehensive understanding of the topic at hand.

Critical books can be written by scholars, academics, experts, and other professionals in the field, covering a wide range of subjects and topics. They often require extensive research and analysis and can be drawn from a range and secondary sources to support your arguments and conclusions. Examples of critical books include literary criticism of novels, philosophical discussions of ethical theories, and scientific studies of historical events or social phenomena. Critical books are often influential in shaping public opinion and academic discourse and can play an important role in advancing knowledge and understanding in various fields of study.

When and where did you meet, the past of her family, love, marriage, the birth of your three children... You have a lot to write about. Eventually her death. There should be more text, more living flesh, impressions, memories, and emotions. You go from an essay to a historical story, from it to photographs, from them to reports, and finally letters from readers. These are contributions of different genres,

---

27   Which are critical books and which are biographies? Why is the review of my manuscript classified into those two types of books?

28   Why should I write my feelings to you?

29   Why not through a medical report? What is missing from the medical report?

which do not go together. You should read more autobiographies and biographies.

◊

Can genre contributions: essays, historical stories, photographs, reports, and letters from readers go together in one book?

Yes, different genres such as essays, historical stories, photographs, reports, and letters from readers can be included in the same book. Many books incorporate multiple genres to create a more varied and interesting reading experience for the audience.

However, it is important to keep in mind that the different genres should be organized in a way that makes sense and flows smoothly for the reader. For example, essays and reports could be grouped together, while historical stories and photographs could be interspersed throughout the book to provide visual interest and break up longer blocks of text.

In addition, the book should have a clear theme or overarching message that connects the different genres. This will help ensure that the book feels cohesive and purposeful, rather than a collection of disparate parts.

Overall, the key is to approach the combination of different genres thoughtfully and intentionally that enhance the reader's experience and add to the overall impact of the book.[30]

---

30   https://chat.openai.com/chat Licenca: CC BY 4.0

CONCLUSION

With this, I gave Sofia more text, more flesh, impressions, and emotions for her excellent evaluation, which she gave. I have provided a detailed and thorough analysis and evaluation of her ideas, arguments, and theories.

Sofia, as the name she bears tells her, wisely and insightfully judges that nothing is right here and that there are mixed frogs and grandmothers, but her "sole hurts" because there are mixed frogs and grandmothers here, and she will not, she is not capable, nor she know how to put frogs in their place and grandmothers in their place.

ABOUT ABORTION

The decision to have an abortion is a deeply personal matter and ultimately depends on the woman who is pregnant. The final decision should always be made by the pregnant woman.

What if there is no medical justification for abortion, but the reasons for the abortion decision are different?

What if a woman does not want and will not include her husband, that is, a man, in the decision-making process?

What if the husband, a man, does not want or would not want his wife, or the woman with whom he is in a relationship, to have an abortion? He is not indifferent and does not care.

The woman decides for herself. All options for abortion are available to her.

What's a husband to do, a man? Feeling distressed, deeply depressed, and left behind? Should he be treated to get out of such and such condition? To pull the hair from his head or to beat himself in the head with his fists? Whether?

What is the role of a man, a husband, in the process of giving birth to a child? Means, a facility for insemination? What is a man, a husband? An erotic aid? As the reader and the author meet on the pages of the book "Life Lift", they talk about "spilled soup and meat that was taken home". In this case, too, was the "soup spilled" somewhere "outside the house"?

A woman, like an adult girl, makes her own decisions on less significant matters. Either they will or they won't. There is no compulsion.

"No woman aborts her child. It aborts other people's."[31] Why should someone else's child in a woman's womb have to be aborted?

How much does an abortion cost? Where does the woman get the money to pay for the abortion?

On the pages of the book, the woman whispers to her beloved, unborn Anta, that he understands her, because others don't, that her life is difficult and that's why she has to deprive him of his life by aborting him. Ante understands her. He will help his mother. Who is he going to help, if not his mother? It is instructive and educational. Ante was taught to help before he was born. Well, my Ante. Bless you for waiting, or not waiting.

---

31   Slavica Perović, „Life Lift", New book, 2012, str.296

SAND DUNE[32]

Before the reader is a very serious and layered text, which requires good concentration, attention, and education.

The author contemplates the abstract concepts of the human soul, spirit, spirituality, consciousness, and mind using scientific literature from Kant to Sigmund Freud, Eric Berne, and others.

The goal is to decipher the "chaotic murmur of human destiny", which, as we see, depends not only on the individual but on the family script, social communities, and systems at the local and global levels. His life experience and the dramatic moment of parting from his beloved being, his beloved Branka, led him to such deep thoughts.

The love we read between the lines of this text is deep and lasting, just as Željko's insight into the "chaotic murmur of human destiny" is also deep.

I would conclude that the author is extremely educated, but also a lyrical soul with an exceptional gift for describing the feeling of solitude, transience, and the ambiance of a small town, as Podgorica used to be and is now.

---

32   Dina Pješčana is a professor of literature and languages

LITERATURE

1. Gabriel García Márquez, "One Hundred Years of Solitude", Joint Edition, Executive Publisher IRO "Education" OOUR "Publishing Activity", Belgrade 1985.

2. Copyright©1998-2022 VREME, Belgrade, *https://www.vreme.com/ projekat/dokumet-spisak-16101- golootocana/* License: CCBY4.0

3. Mihail Jurjevič Lermontov, "Hero of our time", "Veselin Masleša", Sarajevo 1974.

4. Slavica Perović, "Life Lift", New book, Podgorica, 2012

5. Fredrik Bakman, "A man named Uve", New book, Podgorica, 2018

6. Hemodialysis-bs.svg, User: YassineMrabet https://commons.wikimedia.org/wiki/File:Hemodialysis-bs.svg License: CC BY 4.0

7. Miljenko Jergović, "Hero of our time/Juraj Lerotić and why a man is never as present and alive as in the moments when someone close to him dies", 08.11.2022.

https://www.jergovic.com/junak-naseg-doba/juraj-lerotic-i-zasto-covjek-nikada-nije-so-present-i-ziv-kao-u-trenucima-kada-mu-netko-close-dying/

8. Gabor Mate, "When the body says no", @Kontrast publishing house. in 2021

9. Igor D. Cvejić, "Kant's theory of feelings" - doctoral dissertation, University of Belgrade, Faculty of Philosophy, Belgrade 2016.

10. "Dictionary of Philosophical Terms", Filozofija.org, (prist.21.01.2023) https://www.filozofija.org/rjecnik-filozofskih-pojmova/

11. "Philosophical Dictionary", Matice Hrvatske Publishing House, Zagreb 1989.

12. Simon Blackburn, "The Oxford Dictionary of Philosophy",

© Oxford University Press 1996

13. Dragan Krstić, "Psychological Dictionary", Contemporary Administration, Belgrade, 1991

14. Vladimir Stanojević, "The Tragedy of Genius", Medical book, Belgrade–Zagreb, 1990.

15. https://chat.openai.com/chat (Accessed 03/01/2023)

16. Psychiatry, Croatian encyclopedia, online edition, Lexicographic Institute Miroslav Krleža 2021, *https://www.enciklopedija.hr/Natuknica. aspx?ID=50915*

(Prist. 02.01.2023)

17. Janse, B. (2021). Psychoanalysis.Retrieved [20.12.2022] from Toolshero*: https://www.toolshero.com/psychoanalysis/*

18. Sigmund Freud, "Complete Introduction to Psychoanalysis", New book, Podgorica, 2019.

19. Todor Baković, "Depressive Optimism of Montenegrins", Publisher "Jugoagent" Zagreb ("Otokar Keršovani" Pula), 1985.

20. Drago Britvić and Arsen Dedić, https://www.youtube.com/ watch?v=0I2ckIXc7Zs License: [Merilin] Croatia Records (on behalf of Croatia Records), and 2 Music Rights Societies, Podgorica, 18.12.2022.

21. Miroslav Rus, Nikša Bratoš, *https://www.youtube.com/ watch?v=VMT50KhLIRw License:* [Merilin]IDJDigital (on behalf of City Records), and 4 Music Rights Societies, License: CC BY 4.0

22. Eric Berne "What game are you playing?", Idavac Ne&Bo, Belgrade, 1998.

23. Eric Bern, "What do you say after hello?", Belgrade: Beoknjiga, 2008.

24. M. Scott Peck, "The Road Less Traveled", Publisher JRJ Zemun, 1993.

25. *https://chat.openai.com/chat (Accessed 27.03.2023)*

THE END

Autumn has passed. The end of winter is approaching. I celebrated my birthday yesterday. He sang a song with his grandchildren: Today is a wonderful day, a wonderful day, our grandfather's birthday. He blew out the candle on the cake.

I approach the window. I move the curtain and look at the same Kindergarten, a grassy yard, various types of pines, three solitaires, and residential buildings in the neighborhood, built in the seventies of the last century. They were made by the apartment factory from Spuz.

I look up. Above the tops of the buildings, you can see the dark green, wooded top of Gorica hill. Behind her, was the Sorcerer, with the top covered with two white clouds. On the left is Brotnjik with snow on top. He is touched by the clouds. Even further to the left, between the solitaires, you can see the Trijebač hill with a monument on top. Behind and above it is the Piper Rock. On the far right are Sjenica's sides. Above all, the sky was covered with gray thick clouds. To the right, towards Kolašin, Bjelasica, and Kuči, the clouds are lighter and transparent.

My literature professor told me not to hyperbolize my Branka.

01.03.2023.

NOTE ABOUT AUTHOR

On the road less traveled

Željko Vujović was born on February 28, 1952 in Podgorica.

He published the following books:

– The Book About Branka (2023)

– Bosnia needs to be passed - Aporias of Elijah of Thunder (2021)

– A small album of memories – excerpts from the biography Torn from Oblivion (2020)

– From Nuclear Spin to Magnetic Resonance Imaging (2019)

– What language did my mother speak? (2018)

– Memory (2017)

He has published scientific articles, of which the following stand out:

– Magnets, Gradients, and RF Coils of MR Scanners (2023)

– Classification Model Evaluation Metrics (2021)

– Big Data and Machine Learning (2020)

– Magnetic Resonance Signal (2019)

He lives in Podgorica